Dear Friend:

You may have noticed that this book is put together differently than most other quality paperbacks. The page you are reading, for instance, along with the back page, is glued to the cover. And when you open the book the spine "floats" in back of the pages. But there's nothing wrong with your book. These features allow us to produce what is known as a detached cover, specifically designed to prevent the spine from cracking even after repeated use. A state-of-the-art binding technology known as OtaBind® is used in the manufacturing of this and all Health Communications, Inc. books.

HCI has invested in equipment and resources that ensure the books we produce are of the highest quality, yet remain affordable. At our Deerfield Beach headquarters, our editorial and art departments are just a few steps from our pressroom, bindery and shipping facilities. This internal production enables us to pay special attention to the needs of our readers when we create our books.

Our titles are written to help you improve the quality of your life. You may find yourself referring to this book repeatedly, and you may want to share it with family and friends who can also benefit from the information it contains. For these reasons, our books have to be durable and, more importantly, user-friendly.

OtaBind® gives us these qualities. Along with a crease-free spine, the book you have in your hands has some other characteristics you may not be aware of:

• Open the book to any page and it will lie flat, so you'll never have to worry about losing your place.

• You can bend the book over backwards without damage, allowing you to hold it with one hand.

• The spine is 3-5 times stronger than conventional perfect binding, preventing damage even with rough handling.

This all adds up to a better product for our readers—one that will last for years to come. We stand behind the quality of our books and guarantee that, if you're not completely satisfied, we'll replace the book or refund your money within 30 days of purchase. If you have any questions about this guarantee or our bookbinding process, please feel free to contact our customer service department at 1-800-851-9100.

We hope you enjoy the quality of this book, and find understanding, insight and direction for your life in the information it provides.

Health Communications, Inc.®

3201 S.W. 15th Street
Deerfield Beach, FL 33442-8190
(305) 360-0909

Peter Vegso
President

LIVING
SIMPLY

Timeless Thoughts
for a
Balanced Life

SARA OREM &
LARRY DEMAREST

Health Communications, Inc.
Deerfield Beach, Florida

Library of Congress Cataloging-in-Publication Data

Orem, Sara
    Living simply: timeless thoughts for a balanced life/Sara Orem & Larry
Demarest.
       p.   cm.
    ISBN 1-55874-321-9 (paper): $9.95
    1. Simplicity. I. Demarest, Larry . II. Title.
BJ1496.O74   1994   94-23548
179'.9—dc20   CIP

©1994 Sara Orem and Larry Demarest
ISBN 1-55874-321-9

All rights reserved. Printed in the United States of America. No part of
this publication may be reproduced, stored in a retrieval system or
transmitted in any form or by any means, electronic, mechanical, pho-
tocopying, recording or otherwise without the written permission of
the publisher.

Publisher: Health Communications, Inc.
          3201 S.W. 15th Street
          Deerfield Beach, Florida 33442-8190

Cover design by Lawna P. Oldfield

Simplicity is a characteristic of mind
and cannot be judged by appearances. It is
an integration, a stability, a settledness,
a straightforwardness, a purity of mind that is
often expressed in a simpler lifestyle—
a simpler diet, a more orderly routine, a more
intelligent use of time, less clutter, less
financial chaos, fewer involvements—
in other words, less world,
more peace.

Hugh Prather

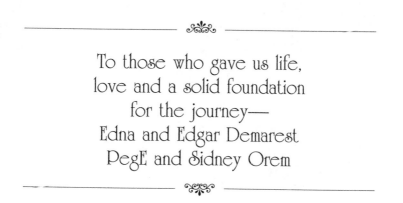

To those who gave us life,
love and a solid foundation
for the journey—
Edna and Edgar Demarest
PegE and Sidney Orem

Contents

Introduction

We two are products of the American culture of the last 50 years. This means we are children of parents who lived through the Depression and the Second World War. Both of our engineer dads worked within organizations that shaped much of their adult lives, and hence our formative years. It means that we grew up with a particular set of expectations about what our adult responsibilities would be but have lived a different reality from the one we expected. It means that we participated in the emancipation of women and others from narrow definitions of what people should be and do.

We each have been single parents and have both faced the challenge of step-parenting. We, like many of the readers of this book, have had splintered families, due both to divorce and geographic distance from parents and siblings. We each have children and careers, community commitments and home maintenance that require continuing attention.

In the last several years we have felt an increasing pull to simplify our lives, for reasons that are probably somewhat different for each of us. Sara chose to change the course of her work life as a result of disillusionment with a high-pressure career in financial services. She took some time out to return to school for a graduate degree in religious studies. Larry left a career in health care education to start a business where he was free to create opportunities that did not exist for him within organizations. While this has meant no less attention to his profession, it has allowed him to shape his own days and to say no to opportunities that are not within his priorities.

We have not chucked our four-bedroom house to move to a one-bedroom cabin in the woods or the desert, although we dream of and plan for that. We still have one child in college with staggering tuition bills. Each of us travels a fair amount in conjunction with our work. And we try to maintain our volunteer commitments.

Although our lives are no less complex, we are heading in a purposeful direction, one that includes more writing, speaking and time alone. We are focused less on income and more on experiencing the people and activities that nurture us. We ask ourselves with each important decision, "Will this add richness to our lives and all life, or is it just one more thing to do?"

We have found that there is a growing number of adults, some of whom have "arrived" and others who are still on the path, who are experiencing the same disillusionment and the desire to move in new directions in their lives. They sense that something fundamental is missing from the effort they were so confident would deliver it all. These same adults are perplexed and often unsure about what to do, but they are voicing their concerns more frequently and may be ready to try something different. *Living Simply* is addressed to these adults who are trying to change their lives by refocusing, rebalancing and simplifying.

The quotations and reflections in *Living Simply* reflect six interconnected themes we hear expressed by those seeking to redirect their lives. They are:

- Choices: Taking responsibility for the course of one's life, often explicitly rejecting society's demands and expectations

- Balance: Rebalancing one's life, typically to reduce the demands of work and to attend instead to important relationships, physical health and/or spiritual development
- Simplicity: Reducing concern for and involvement with material goods because life is about people, not things
- Vocation: Engaging in work that makes a distinct contribution to society and closely reflects one's identity while assisting in the development of that identity
- Harmony: Recognizing the interconnectedness of all life and the impact of one's lifestyle on the earth, the lives of other people and other creatures
- Wisdom: Accepting and experiencing life as a process of change and development, and gathering the lessons learned along life's journey.

We have written about these themes as much to remind ourselves to stay focused on the important people and visions in our lives as to share any lessons we may have learned along the way. Our sincere hope is that you will find support and nourishment in *Living Simply* for your own journeys toward simplicity and that you will share your learnings with us.

Sara Orem
Larry Demarest

Choices

1

Choices

A friend I've known well over the years tells a story on himself about lying in bed one beautiful weekend morning struggling with a decision—should he get up and ride his bike around the lake near his apartment, or should he stay there and read TIME Magazine? The story always gets a laugh, at least when my friend tells it. What difference could it make for Charlie to have done one thing or the other? And yet I suspect that most of us are caught occasionally in our own version of this indecision. Should I take this new job, or stay in the job I have? Should I marry this person or remain single, or marry another? Should I go to graduate school or flip hamburgers? And if I do, then what?

I spend the weekend with a couple I know and love very much. For as long as they have been married the wife has asked, "Should I stay in this marriage or not?" From my vantage point this indecision must be hard on both of them, yet they continue to choose to remain married.

Responsibility seems to me to be about making those decisions, those choices, and then living out the consequences, accepting that we made the best choices we could at the time. Making choices includes the care and consideration of the consequences beforehand: What might happen? How can I best pursue this? Who should I ask? What do I need to know?

At some point, this process must include movement, movement toward the decision or choice. Some of us never seem to get to the movement part. For all kinds of reasons (usually having to do with our responsibilities toward or for another) we say, "I don't have any choice." Even when we have been offered opportunities that are obvious to those we love, we continue to opt for no choice, for indecision or for no decision.

In a recent job transition, a professional colleague suggested that the most difficult decisions we face are usually about 50/50 in terms of what is to be gained. A decision one way seems to have about 50 percent of the advantages and a decision the other way seems to have about the same percentage. What makes the difference, my colleague says, is our own commitment. When we commit to one side of that 50 percent, the scale is tipped and we are able to make our decision work.

During a time when I was having difficulty with a decision I had made, another wise friend suggested to me that I could like my decision without liking the consequences of that decision. Wow! Did that help! I had made a good decision. But the decision meant I was alone, in economic insecurity, jobless and afraid. Some consequences! I needed long-term commitment to make that decision work.

Taking responsibility for choosing can also mean that we are not satisfied with the choice we've made and need to make another decision or choice. I went to graduate school a few years ago to become a minister. Within months of starting my studies I knew that ordained ministry was the wrong choice for me. After having told my family, my friends, my boss and my former colleagues that I would see them at the altar, I had to re-choose even though I had been certain that I wanted to pursue ordination six months before.

The big responsibilities are sometimes easier than the less significant ones. It's easy to understand that marriage or divorce are serious choices with long-term consequences. Deciding to quit my job in order to pursue another career had serious implications for our family's financial stability.

But what of the more ambiguous choices? Does it really matter if I claim expenses I didn't incur on my expense account? Do the little lies I tell in my primary relationship really erode mutual trust if my mate doesn't know I'm lying? What about overspending or overeating?

Responsibility based on the value of simplicity guides the small choices as well as the large ones. I don't cheat on my expense account because I value honesty and trustworthiness, but it's also simpler. I don't lie to my husband because I value the mutual trust we have built, but it's also simpler. I do often overeat and overspend and the consequences just fill my life with extra weight to drag around and extra stuff to store.

We write about responsibility, about making choices, because one of those choices, the choice to attempt to live more simply, has guided many of the other decisions we have made in our marriage and professional lives. But we have a long way to go.

Simplicity doesn't always provide clear guidance. It probably wouldn't have helped Charlie decide whether to read or
ride his bike. But it does help to refine, to clarify, to reduce
to essentials the elements of many responsibilities we weigh
and many of the choices we choose. It is one way to reduce
the physical and psychological clutter of the complex life we
once chose, and to some degree still do. It is one way to re-
choose another path.

It takes courage to commit to your
own deepest desires. . . .

Robert and Marilyn Kriegel

Many children are encouraged to take their hopes and dreams seriously. "You can do anything you want" is what many of us heard from Mom and Dad and other adults in our lives.

Over time this support erodes. "How could you leave a perfectly good job?" my friend's mother asked when he resigned his "secure" government position to pursue an opportunity that was important to him. The message is clear: it is okay to have dreams as a child, but adults who take their dreams seriously are not taken seriously themselves.

Yet it is often precisely these adults—those who commit to their own visions—who thrive in life and end up getting where they really want to go. They do not deny reality (by counting on winning a lottery or trying to run a marathon after being sedentary for years), but they do press on toward the distantly possible with commitment and passion, even though others may shake their heads in disbelief.

Even when others doubt, I can
summon the courage to take my deepest hopes
and dreams seriously. In fact, to live fully
I must take them seriously.

--------------------------------- ❧ ---------------------------------

*In many ways it has always been easier
to act as if there were not options;
as if we didn't have a choice.*

                                                    Amy Saltzman

--------------------------------- ❧ ---------------------------------

When we took our first steps on the path to adulthood, we may not have realized that we had choices. As we chose work, a mate and a place to live, we may have been thinking within narrow limits and presumed that the path always led upward, from an entry level position to ones with increasing responsibility and importance; from a modest, struggling salary to comfort; from a small dwelling to one with ample space and grounds. It may even have felt as though we didn't actively choose those things, but that they just appeared on the path.

This path took many of us to a place where we believed we no longer had a choice, where we felt trapped, locked in. When we say things like, "What choice do I really have?" or, "I'd really like to but . . ." we are conditioning ourselves to continue to believe and act as though we are choiceless, when what we really mean is "I feel obligated to . . ." or "I do not want to risk . . ." or "I choose to continue to maintain my current comfort level."

But we do have choices: choices regarding everything from the kind of packaging we purchase, to whether we walk or drive, to how much of our lives we give to our jobs. And we always have a choice about the words we say and about our attitude.

Believing that we always have a choice—that for the most part we are in charge—is a cornerstone of the journey toward balance, renewal and simplicity.

*I am grateful that I have choices, and I will exercise
them to sustain and enhance my life.*

❧
Success is such an enticing word.

Thomas F. Crum
❧

Success in our culture is typically understood to mean a certain level of achievement, often shown through material abundance, public acclaim or social and occupational prominence. Part of its enticement comes when we are acknowledged and reinforced for being superior in these ways. Much in our organizational and social lives assumes that these kinds of success are what motivate people.

We are less likely to be recognized for being a successful mate or parent, or successfully reducing our material needs or establishing a regular meditation time, although these achievements may be more fundamental, enduring and connected to life.

To communicate our motivations to others as well as to ourselves, we need to reclaim "success" and cast it in a broader light. It is okay to be enticed by success at living in harmonious balance with ourselves, our loved ones and other life.

I can define "success" for me and be
pleased to call myself "successful"
on my own terms.

I would like it to be different,
but it can't be now.

Henri Nouwen

There are two things I would like to be different in my life now. One is my weight and the other is how I use my morning time. I would like my weight to be less and I would like to use early morning, especially in the spring and summer, for meditation, prayer and writing.

At least that is what I say I'd like to change. In particular, I say these things when I have just finished eating and when it is not early morning. When I have the choice to take specific actions that would support these changes, I seem to choose other results. When snack food is available, I eat it, even when there are other foods such as fruits and vegetables. When I awake at 6 a.m., I roll over, doze for awhile and then read the paper before I set about my day. Later in the day I sometimes wonder why I haven't written as much as I'd like or when I'll ever find time for prayer.

I want things to be different, but apparently not now. But now is the only time I have to begin to make it different. It is what I say, do and believe now that will determine whether I lose weight, spend more time meditating and writing, and begin taking other definite steps on the path I say I want to travel. If I truly want things to be different, it has to be now.

Today I will do one thing that moves
me toward where I want to be.

--- ❦ ---

Simplicity may be difficult, but the alternative
is immensely more difficult.

Richard J. Foster

--- ❦ ---

Simplicity difficult—really. I would have thought that simplicity
would be . . . well, you know . . . simple.

Of course, I haven't really tried simplicity, so I guess I'd have to
say that I don't know. I have tried the alternative; we all have. And
yes, that does seem to be quite difficult. Frustrating, exhausting,
emptying, distracting, all-consuming. It gets so you hardly ever get
to do what you want—work 5 or 6 days a week for a little time for
yourself. Not that it really matters because most of the time I'm not
sure I even know what I want anymore.

Come on. What choice do I really have? What would you do?
You have to pay the mortgage and the bills and buy food and go to
the movies once in awhile. I know there are people who claim you
have choices about everything, and that if you do what you really
want—what really lights your fire deep down inside you—everything else will fall in line.

Hey, who do they think they're kidding? If you really do what
you want, you stand a good chance of becoming a laughingstock
and going bankrupt to boot. But you know, some people do get to
do what they want. I don't know how—maybe they're just lucky. It
could be the law of averages, like a few people are really tall, and
a few people are really smart—a few people get to do what they
want. Most of us working folks have to load our 16 tons before we
can even think about what we'd like to do. The way I see it, if
you're fortunate you get to do what you want in retirement.

Today will be a great day if I don't have to
listen to someone who wants to give me a sermon
about how I really can get what I want in life.

❦

Simplicity . . . is a characteristic of mind
that cannot be judged by appearances. It is an
integration, a stability, a settledness, a
straightforwardness, a purity of the mind that is
often expressed in a simpler life-style—a simpler
diet, a more orderly routine, a more intelligent
use of time, less clutter, less financial chaos,
fewer involvements—in other words, less
world and more peace.

Hugh Prather

At some point we have all yearned to lead a simple life. When you yearn for simplicity, what are you yearning for? To live in the country and "get away from it all"? To be able to concentrate your energy on something important to you? To escape the pressures of daily living and the feeling that everything is your responsibility? To find some time to relax and be happy?

The exciting (and fearful) reality is that we can have that kind of life if we are willing to take some clear steps toward creating it for ourselves.

But it isn't going to drop into our laps just because we want it. Such a life requires discipline of choice in how we use our time, what we eat, the work we choose, how we earn and spend our money, what we say "yes" and "no" to.

And like life itself, simplicity is a journey, not a destination. We won't necessarily know when we have arrived, but we will know we are on the path when we have "less world and more peace."

I recognize that simplicity is a state of mind that flows
from the choices and activities of each day.

---

*Do not use the word "can't" when
you actually mean "won't."*

John D. Adams

Language is powerful. The way we talk about people and things affects our attitudes and behavior toward them and helps to create our reality. Saying "can't" establishes limits for ourselves and helps to create a reality where we have less power and fewer options and where we may feel locked in.

On the other hand, saying "won't" establishes us as active players, reflecting a reality where we feel free to say what we want and don't want, where we make choices instead of having them dictated to us.

Sometimes, of course, "can't" is the appropriate word. We can't turn back the clock and undo something that has occurred. We can't supersede human limits or disregard the laws of nature.

But we often use "can't" when we mean "won't." Have you ever said "I can't find the time" when you meant "I won't make it a priority right now," or "I can't get away" when you meant "I choose not to attend"? Have you ever said "I can't change jobs," "I can't communicate with my mate," "I can't . . ."?

An acquaintance has described with some pain the sense of dread and burnout he feels in his job, especially as he looks ahead to the five years he has until retirement. He adds, "But nothing can be done, that's just the way it is. I have a family to think of."

If he were really thinking of his family, wouldn't he be better off taking action to improve his situation, to take care of himself? He could change his job responsibilities, take an extended time off, even seek a totally new position within the large organization where he works (and his boss has indicated support for any of these!), but he says he can't. For a complicated web of reasons, he won't.

*I will try to say "can't" when I mean "can't"
and "won't" when I mean "won't."*

Son: "I don't want to leave the beach."
Father: "Neither do I, son! But growing up means
doing a lot of things we don't want to do!"
Son: "That's dumb! You and Mom could get jobs here!
We could get a house here!"
Husband to wife: "You'd better talk to him!"

Jimmy Johnson, creator of Arlo 'N' Janis

Is this son naive, or does he hit the nail right on the head? Could the family really live at the beach if they wanted to or do the hard realities of life dictate otherwise?

Certainly many adults would give this father's response. We encourage our children to be children while they can because they will face adult responsibilities soon enough. A fundamental reality of that adult world is that you don't get to do what you really want, at least not very often.

That sense of being "determined" rather than being a "determiner" frequently carries over to our life and work styles. We would like to simplify our lives and restore balance to them, but the demands of a career, the expectations of family and our own sense of who we are stand in the way. What we forget (or deny) is that we chose to live and work as we do, and that we can choose other ways.

Making such choices may have both positive and negative consequences: that's why we call them choices. Living at the beach may provide a more relaxing setting with more time spent in renewing recreation or enjoying nature. It might also mean a smaller house, a longer commute, a job change, living on less income. So while living at the beach would provide a lot, it would also have its costs. But the costs do not make it an impossible choice.

I acknowledge that I can choose to "stay at the beach."

People either have results in their lives
or the reasons why they don't.

from the business card of Bonnie Andrkopoulos

I want to lose weight and eat a low-fat diet, but the last few months have been full of parties and special occasions, and I have been working hard and have found it difficult to eat properly when my schedule is disrupted and I am under stress. I also want to set aside a regular quiet time for meditation and renewal, but my schedule does not allow it. The few times I have been able to find the time I have been interrupted.

In these areas of my life, I have reasons, not results.

How about you—are you living your reasons or living your results?

When people talk about their reasons, their stories sound so convincing, especially to themselves. When I listen I too understand why it couldn't be any other way for them.

But then I encounter others who have successfully dealt with similar barriers. Though it took some time, my friend Nancy has established a meditation time for herself. It required discipline on her part, and it took some effort for everyone in her family (including the pets) to respect that time. She too had her reasons—not wanting to get up so early, young children who required attention, a spouse who didn't understand at first—but now she has her result.

I really want to write a book, but . . . hey, I guess I have. Maybe I have started to run out of reasons.

I can trade in my "reasons"
for the results I seek.

❦

If you want something to happen,
make a space for it.

David Campbell

❦

Do you remember a time when experts were concerned about how we would use all the leisure time that shorter work weeks and labor-saving devices would provide us? I do, but that time simply has not come to anyone I know. We are all suffering from busyness. Even retired people have full plates.

So when a new idea, even a good idea, an important idea, comes along, we naturally wonder how we will fit it in. Exercise, journalling, family and friends, spiritual practice, serving others, even learning to cook in more healthy ways all take time; all add something to our already overflowing plates. How can we do it, how can we possibly add yet another activity to our full lives?

When we want something new in our lives, when we want to grow in new ways, we have to make space. Not a lot, at first. But a space nevertheless. And for something new to appear on our plates, something that is already there must be moved aside.

Moving some things aside—examining our busyness and replacing it with basic, life-sustaining and life-enhancing activities—is at the core of living simply and in balance. It is not easy, because every time we choose something we discard something else, but it can be a wonderfully liberating activity. When we move geographically we often discard the unnecessary things we have accumulated so that we can have a fresh start. That is what it means to make space, to make room for a fresh start on a new leg of the journey.

I can make space for something important
to fit into my life.

Know thyself.

Socrates

Recently my son was packing to return to college. At least that was what he was supposed to be doing. What he was actually doing was rummaging through his things, pondering and reminiscing, reading old letters and examining his art work, much like he did when he was younger and supposedly cleaning his room.

Although he wanted to go back to college, the actual packing and moving of all his belongings and readjusting to living in a different place were difficult, and he avoided them as long as he could.

I wanted to say something pointed yet clever, like, "You'll never get to Dallas by taking the road to Tulsa," that would make clear to him that he was caught in one of the mega-patterns of his life, the pattern of saying he wants one thing but doing something apparently contradictory.

Instead I shook my head to myself and puzzled about how anyone could deliberately act like that. Besides, I needed to get on with my own pressing concerns, as I was behind in my writing.

Despite needing to catch up, I didn't write anything that evening. Instead I dozed on my bed under the guise of watching educational television and reading magazines, all the while wondering how my son could shoot himself in the foot in the next room.

It wasn't until several days later that I realized that I had been doing the same thing my son had been doing, and that focusing on him had diverted my attention from my own behavior.

We cannot begin to change until we see our own proclivities, until we know ourselves not as we would like to be, but as we really are.

Holding a mirror up to my own behavior
will help me know myself.

Many of us go through life not clear about what
we want but pretty sure this isn't it.

Janet Hagberg and Richard Leider

Today I am sure of what I do not want and it is what I have. It is a day when it feels like I am being pulled in a thousand directions. It is a day when the line at the post office is longer than I've seen it for months and all the people in front of me have complicated transactions. It is a day when I spend a lot of time and energy on less productive work, while neglecting projects that are higher priority. Oh yes, I know what I don't want!

When I get to this place in my life, I begin to send myself little signals. Actually they aren't little signals, they are big signals, red flags. One of the red flags is saying to myself, "I don't want to live this way; I don't want to work this way." I said that to myself recently as I rushed to the airport without a second to spare in my schedule.

Fortunately I have arrived at the point in life where I also know what I do want. Because I am self-employed, I have a fair amount of latitude and discretion to move myself in that direction.

In the past, I would allow myself to stay stuck when I reached that point of frustration. Now I am aware of things to do to move myself. One is to be patient. For instance, this week culminates a particularly busy month, but as I look ahead my calendar has some breaks in it. Another is to be more deliberate about where I put my time and energy by making commitments that allow me to say, "This is the way I want to live."

I rejoice knowing that I choose to
move toward what I want.

Before you can take care of anyone or anything, you
must first take care of yourself.

Spencer Johnson

I remember very clearly the first time someone said that I should
take care of myself. A counselor suggested it to me during a coun-
seling session. I also remember my reaction. I thought that taking
care of myself was a selfish act, that if I had wanted to be on my
own I wouldn't have chosen to be married and have children, that
in a family people are interdependent and care for one another,
they don't "take care of themselves."

Over the years I have come to a very different understanding of
that idea, and it has been an important part of my growth as an adult.

I now know that I become stressed-out, cranky and unfocused
when I am tired, when I don't eat right, when I don't exercise, when
I don't take the time to enjoy my hobbies. Thus I am less able to be
a good speaker and writer, a good consultant, a good husband, a
good father and a good friend. When I feel that way I also don't
have a very good relationship with myself.

It makes perfect sense that we need to be healthy and happy and
focused before we can be of service to others, before we can help
anyone else or care for anything. Rather than being a selfish act, taking care of myself is actually the first step toward caring for others.

I affirm that taking care of myself is a basic part
of being interdependent with others.

What are the nonnegotiable elements of your life?
What are the things you absolutely must have
and do so that you can feel that you have
lived your life and not wasted it?

Harold Kushner

For many adults the transition from young adulthood to the responsibilities of marriage, family, career and community has meant giving up things that were important to us. I remember when my first child was born, I gave up playing football on Saturday morning with friends because I needed to be at home.

It took me awhile to realize that I had entered a long period of giving up. I gave up football (playing football was not one of the nonnegotiable parts of my life, but, as it turned out, having time for friends and for exercise was), I gave up camping, I gave up time for reading and reflecting. The loss of any one of these was not a loss that I could not overcome. But the impact of their collective loss was serious. After years of giving up the things that were important and nourishing to me, I reached a point where I realized I had abandoned many of the most vital and nurturing activities in my life.

We often identify and negotiate our nonnegotiable demands only with ourselves. People did not ask me to give up the things I was giving up. I had decided on my own that it was necessary; I believed that giving up certain activities was just part of being an adult.

What's nonnegotiable—what's important to us that gives meaning and balance to our lives—is different at different times. So we can expect the particulars to change as we change. But our determination to have them should not waver.

I will negotiate with myself to maintain those activities
that let me know I am living the life I want to live.

... people on their death beds don't say,
"Gee, I wish I'd spent more time at the office."
They say, "I wish I'd spent more time with my wife
or my kids, or exploring nature."

Mark Gerzon

When I use that quote in a talk, people usually laugh. Yet we all know it is not funny; many of us know people who lived and died that way. We may be existing that way ourselves, spending so much time on one endeavor that we seriously shortchange others.

People in the United States work more hours per week now than at any time since the end of World War II. We work more and have less time off than those in most of the industrialized world (except Japan). Many people feel as though they have reached the end of their ropes, the physical and psychological limits of being able to do more with less. Other parts—important parts—of our lives cannot help but be ignored when so much of our time and energy go to our employment.

I know what I want to do now to avoid that scenario when I reach the end of my days. I want to spend more time writing, taking pictures, watching birds, nurturing satisfying relationships, staying healthy, developing spiritual practices and helping others.

To what do you want to devote more time and attention? What is it that you want to do now so that when you reach your death bed you can say, "I wanted to spend more time _____ and I did and I'm glad"?

*I will arrange my life so that I can spend
more time _____.*

---

*We are the doorways of life and we must choose
what comes in and what goes out.*

Marge Piercy

How often does the choice get lost in the coming in and the going out? A full calendar testifies to our busyness, but does it also testify to our commitment? Can we remember why we serve on the board of this organization or write the article for that newsletter? Is it because those tasks provide labels, ways in which we are known and are important to others? Or is it because we feel passionately about the work of the organization on whose board we serve or passion for the cause about which we've been asked to write?

If we are to be doorways, we must stand purposefully around the choices we make. We must choose those things that use our highest talents, fill our hearts with deep emotion, bring meaning to our lives and let us share ourselves with the world. If we are but calendar fillers, we won't have the time, or the stamina, or the attention to give to those choices that provide ultimate meaning for our individual and communal lives.

*Do I fill my doorway with things to do, or do I choose
the comings in and the goings out that enhance
the meaning and peace in my life?*

There ain't no answer. There ain't going to be any answer. There never has been an answer. That's the answer.

Gertrude Stein

Children are given answers by parents and grandparents, teachers and other children. "Why is the sky blue, Mommy?" "Why did God forget to say 'honor thy children' when God said 'honor thy parents'?" Adults may struggle to adequately answer the BIG questions children ask, such as, "Who is God?" or, "Why do we have wars?"

As children become adults, they find that the answers they've been provided don't necessarily fit with their experience. Wise guides and mentors encourage children and young adults to find their own answers.

When we look to books and inspirational speakers (answers that work for other people) instead of asking ourselves, our own deep knowing, what the answers are for us, we limit ourselves and risk the possibility of attaching ourselves to someone else's dream.

Just as every human being is physically different, so each person's answer to life's meaning is individual. Find your own answer. That's the answer.

—————————————— ✿ ——————————————

Not every giving of our word to another is an
unlimited yielding of an unlimited claim.

Margaret Farley

—————————————— ✿ ——————————————

Commitment is important. Honoring commitment to important persons, contracts, ideas and hopes honors our deepest selves. But sometimes the nature of the contract, or more important, the nature of ourselves, changes. It is then important to rethink the commitment in light of what has changed in our lives.

When a spouse dies, or a parent moves, or a child goes to college, our relationship to them frequently suggests a change in commitments. It may not make sense to continue to go to Mom's for the holidays if Mom has moved a thousand miles farther away, even though you and Mom thought you would always come to her place for special occasions. Perhaps you will move out of the house you and your partner loved, and to which you committed so much of your energy, when your partner is no longer there.

At these times reassessing the commitments you choose to honor is important. At all of these crossroads simplifying is an option. Would you be happier with less? A less responsible job may mean you would have more time to read or travel. A smaller home would take less time to repair and maintain. Simpler meals may free up a stressful schedule or a stretched waistband. A walk in the woods fills your lungs and your mind with fresh air, exposing natural loveliness as well as intellectual creativity.

The rules we live by need dusting off occasionally.
Sometimes crisis blows the dust off. We don't
need crisis to ask, "Do I still want this?
Would I be happier without it?"

The voice of the soul speaks in loving
ways and not in "shoulds."

Diane Mariechild

Many of us have an inner voice that drives us. That voice does not call for rest or pleasure. It rarely speaks in gentle tones. The voice may belong to a parent long dead or a religious figure whose judgment consumes us.

Where did the voice come from? Have we always heard it? Is the voice ever satisfied with the way we are in the world? We alone have the power to change the voice. It may be helpful to imagine the voice as a record or an audiotape, some visual mechanism that has a switch or a button. When the voice upbraids us, when words such as "stupid" or "not good enough" ring in our ears, we can imagine ourselves turning the voice off. Push the button. Eject the tape. Stop.

Observe the silence. If the voice proceeds, push the button again.

A way of life can only be chosen when it is our way. Not the way our father told us it should be. Not the way we may have been taught in religious school. The way we choose. We can choose to create a new voice, the voice of gentleness for ourselves. The voice of our soul.

Turn off the words of judgment and listen
to the silence. The voice of your soul
will come gently, lovingly.

All those who through history have helped life
to enlarge, to diversify—at their peril, always at
their peril—have been strongly individual.

Florida Scott-Maxwell

Our society provides strong incentive to fit into the mainstream, to get along with each other. From our earliest recollections we are members of groups. We belong to families, we attend school classes, we play on teams and we work in departments.

It is, to some degree, important that we learn to do and be what the group decides is acceptable. In some families it is okay to drink out of the milk carton; in others, this is a major offense. Some children must learn crazy and confusing family rules to survive, while others seem to grow up with consistent nurturing and admiration no matter what they do.

There comes a time for each of us, however, when the group no longer holds so much power or interest. This happens to some people very early on. They learn to dance to their own tune while keeping time to the group's. They function in society, but never seem to be a part of it. Others struggle with meeting their own needs (hearing their tune distinctly and bending to it) versus satisfying the expectations of others (filtering out the other tunes).

There is no right or wrong about this. The tune is always there. The group is always there in one form or another. If we are to truly understand ourselves we will listen to the tune. We will find a time and a place to practice dancing. Eventually we may sing it out loud or learn to play it on an instrument as we dance. This is our gift to the world.

I make time on a regular basis
to listen to my tune.

*The place that is clearest is not necessarily
the place of greatest reality.*

William V. Pietsch

Have you ever faced a decision when the right course of action seemed absolutely clear, but something inside you kept you from making that decision? Perhaps your dad knowingly suggested a job possibility for you. It made good sense. You had the qualifications. But the job didn't seem right somehow. Perhaps you want to leave a job, travel the world, have a baby. The right way (could it be the way our culture would most surely support you?) is clear. But the way of your heart or your intuition is your reality.

Reality is not what somebody else believes is right. What is right for somebody else isn't even always right for them, let alone for you. The path of least resistance may prove to be the hardest path if it does not lead to a place you want to be.

Each of us must decide what reality is for us. We must also decide what we want reality to be and to move in the direction of that reality. Our heart's fulfillment does not necessarily include having a new car every two years. But it might include running a dude ranch or playing the piano. If they are to be reality and not visualization or fantasy, we must take real action toward our dreams. No one else can act for you, although others might argue against what you act for.

*Only I know what my reality is.
Therefore I must act to achieve and sustain it.*

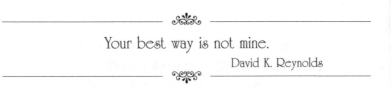

Your best way is not mine.

David K. Reynolds

I wish I could just give you the formula for living a fulfilling, peaceful and balanced life. It would make things much easier, wouldn't it? You wouldn't have to read all these meditations. You could save a lot of time skipping approaches that ultimately will not work. You could just get on with it.

I can't give you a formula because the simple life is a journey, not a destination, and the paths we take are individual. Some folks' journeys lead them out of the rat race and away from urban environments, while others find inner peace and simplicity in the midst of the busiest city. Some find they must leave careers that detract from balance, while others create ways to be balanced in very stressful and competitive environments.

When we are living simply, we are being true to ourselves, and we are involved in activities that fulfill us and make a contribution to something beyond ourselves. This journey requires that we know what we want and what we have to contribute, that we have the courage to stay the course during challenging times, and that we be aware of the effects our way of life has on other living things.

What I have learned may help you and what you have learned may assist me. But I do not know where your path should lead any more than you know where mine should lead. And so the best I can do is support you on your path and ask you to encourage me on mine.

I will learn from others while
setting my own course.

⁂

*Simplicity does not seek the security of things
but opens the soul to both the vulnerability
and wonder of creation.*

Michael Hechmer

⁂

Living simply is not easy. The goal of simplicity calls us to turn away from the goals of much of our culture. Living simply may call us to draw away from family members and long-held associations with friends and neighbors. It may mean giving up (or giving away) things and ways of being we have enjoyed or at least not examined very carefully.

At the very least, living more simply means being more intentional about everything. Can I still spend the money for season tickets to the opera if I also want to work at something that uses more of my creativity but pays me less? Does home mean the comfortable, but now too large, space I have lived in for ten years?

Even those things I know I want to give up, such as cutting the grass and shoveling the snow, have implications for giving up things I do want, such as privacy and space. I now feel vulnerable to the wonders and terrors of creation in a way I did not when I spent most of my time thinking about the next promotion, the next acquisition or the next dinner party. I want to spend more time noticing and being vulnerable to all of creation. I had not realized I would grieve the life I have chosen to simplify.

*There is sadness as well as joy in the
act of simplifying my life.*

--------------------- ❧ ---------------------

In a world of appearances, be sure to
weigh the underlying substance.

Stephen C. Paul

--------------------- ❧ ---------------------

Style is an important word in our culture. Oh, some would say they pay no attention to style. Perhaps there are some who flaunt inattention. But for most of us, some attention to stylish norms is a given. While I don't care if my home reflects the latest color scheme preference, salmon and mist, or some such nonsense, I do care whether my suits and shoes reflect an awareness of fashion. Even my husband, who cares much less than I do, will occasionally ask if some long beloved sweater or pair of trousers is okay to wear in some circumstance.

I don't think it is wrong to care about how we appear to others. I do think it is wrong to care too much. When appearance becomes more important than substance, and we all know people for whom style is substance, then kindness and grace are only affectations on the way to a perceived social summit. This sounds pious and self-congratulatory, so let me say I am not immune to caring more about how I am perceived than how I am. I will often worry more about what I am going to wear to a presentation than what I am going to say. This is my journey too.

Wisdom and grace may wear strange
clothes and live in old houses.

How you live your life is your
true spiritual practice.

Stephen C. Paul

Think of the great spiritual leaders of all time—Confucious, Mohammed, Jesus, and more recently Martin Luther King, Mohandis Gandhi. It was the example of their lives and what they learned in them that gave their teachings such power. Yet living consciously by our values every moment takes some pretty potent commitment and attention.

If we want to be known for what is really important to us, we must live this way. But notice that Paul writes that living is spiritual practice, not achievement of perfection. Life is practice. Unfortunately it is the nature of the human animal not to achieve perfection. It might even be the nature of us not to agree on what perfection is. But each of us has an idea of what that perfect state would look like, and we choose, either consciously or unconsciously, to practice it.

*The intentional practice of our core values is as
close as humans can get to perfection.*

---------------------------------- ❧ ----------------------------------

A seed planted in the ground produces
the fruit of its own kind. . . .What will my seeds be?
What will I choose to plant in the
fertile soil of my life?

Unity's Spiritual Preparation for Easter

I am the caretaker of my inner garden. It is spring. The soil has warmed and I have prepared it. It is waiting to do its job—providing just the right conditions for the sprouting and flowering of seeds.

What seeds shall I plant? What do I want to see push up in the spring, bear fruit and flower in the summer, be harvested in the fall and carry me through the winter? Shall they be seeds of

optimism,
active hope,
love,
peace,
joy,
fun,
fulfillment,
mystery,
balance?

Shall I plant these in my mind so they will show up in my life?

I will sow the seeds I need to
sustain me on my way.

Pick battles big enough to matter,
small enough to win.

Jonathon Kozol

Working late one evening to finish something I definitely needed for the next day, I happened to glance down at the box sitting
under my desk. I thought, "I bet it would only take a few minutes
to clean out that box and throw it away."

At that moment I "forgot" that the box had been sitting unneed-
ed under my desk for quite some time. Why on earth did I think
that cleaning it out would be a good use of my time? Fortunately, I
just as quickly realized that an easily winnable but totally unimpor-
tant battle was vying against one that was quite important and
seemed unwinnable for the moment. I had a laugh at myself and
finished my work.

In a world of infinite time and energy, we could take time for all
battles, great and small. But in our world of finite time and
resources, we are challenged many times each day to choose
among worthwhile alternatives. Let us choose those activities that
really matter to us.

I choose endeavors that will help
me and others win.

I have studied many times
The marble which was chiseled for me—
A boat with a furled sail at rest in a harbor.
In truth it pictures not my destination
But my life. . . .
Ambition called to me, but I dreaded the chances.

Edgar Lee Masters

I don't think it was exactly ambition that called to me. Maybe it was peace or justice, or a calling to take a big risk, or an opportunity to begin to live and work the way I had been saying I wanted to.

I've had my chances, haven't you? I often found them intriguing possibilities—things I might do someday or that would be nice to do if only. They were enticing, but I didn't step up to embrace and seize them.

One day while writing reflections for this book, it hit me that I really could have the life I had been saying for years that I wanted. I really could move to the setting I have desired and craft the kind of day I have envisioned. To do so would require taking action to make it happen, and accepting that both risks and giving up are part and parcel of making the gains I had dreamed of.

That was an exhilarating and scary thought that I didn't hang on to for too long.

*As the captain of my boat, I need to make it
ready and sail it from the harbor.*

Why should we not meet, not always as
dyspeptics, to tell our bad dreams, but sometimes
as eupeptics, to congratulate each other on
the ever-glorious morning? I do not make
an exorbitant demand, surely.

Henry David Thoreau

No, it is not "an exorbitant demand" to greet the day and one another as "glorious" opportunities to share, enjoy and create—to be optimistic instead of pessimistic. In fact, many would claim that there are tangible benefits to be gained by being "eupeptic."

For some this seems to come naturally, although I suspect that a few actually work hard at being optimistic, hopeful and upbeat. For at least one person I know it is a deliberate practice, a kind of ministry.

For others, being "eupeptic" will require changing their routine, for it has become a habit for them to bring the bad news, to complain and to focus on the negative. These are the folks who, when you sing out "Good morning," respond with something like "What's wrong with you," as though sharing the "ever-glorious morning" is some kind of affront, some violation of their right to be miserable. These folks do not add much to a beautiful morning—or the rest of the day for that matter.

Have a nice day, Mr. Thoreau.

---

*The decisions of the past have already
decided your tomorrow.*

Richard Rohr

I spent a part of my work life starting and then evaluating various pilot programs in a college. The idea was to see if the new programs helped, and then to keep them if they did or scuttle them if they proved to be ineffective. One of the things I learned was that it is often harder to stop something than it is to start it. This is as true for individuals and their habits as it is for organizations and societies, as those who have personal habits they wish they could alter will attest.

Some of our decisions, such as making a lifelong commitment to another person or having children, have dramatic impact on our tomorrows and are complicated—or impossible—to untie. Others, such as where we live or how we eat, seem more under our control but difficult to modify nonetheless.

In either case, it is wise to be careful what you start because it is often easier not to start something than it is to undo it later.

*What I am choosing today is
shaping my tomorrows.*

Make a bet every day, otherwise you might
walk around lucky and never know it.

Jimmy Jones

I am not a betting person. But I like the sense of this quotation. It says to me that I should look for the unexpected each day, otherwise I might not see beauty, love, courage, graciousness and fun even when they are right under my nose.

Spring is coming to our state and I look forward to hearing the birds sing their joyous spring songs when I walk to the bus stop in the morning. It took several weeks for me to recognize the new spring songs. (I wouldn't know the singing was indeed different if my bird-watching husband had not pointed out the difference in a cardinal's spring song in our early years together.) Now I expect to hear the difference in the songs and I do.

In some sense, betting is like expecting the bird's spring song. Most of the things we bet about will happen to someone, sooner or later. The birds will begin to sing their melodious song sometime in February. When I listen for the songs, I feel so expectant about their implications. Spring is coming. How lucky for our world.

*Expect to find love, laughter, spring . . .
and you will find them.*

2

Balance

O n the playground as a child, balancing on the seesaw was a challenge. Not the going up and down from one side to the other—that wasn't too difficult as long as the other person weighed about as much as I did. But balancing—staying in the middle—that was the challenge. I was tall and skinny and had long legs and I can remember reaching down with the tips of my toes to just barely push off so that a playmate and I could stay balanced in the middle.

Most of you can remember another part of being on the teeter-totter, a part that was scary. That was when you were suspended high (well it sure seemed high then, didn't it?) in the air by the weight of your mate on the other end. You weren't in balance at all and you were afraid that the person on the other end would jump off unexpectedly and you would crash to the ground.

Perhaps this image reflects some of the challenge of balance that we face. Often, and for long periods of time, we are way out of balance at one end, e.g., working too much, not exercising at all. Then suddenly and with some jarring, we go to the other end, e.g., taking a three-day weekend where we resolve to do nothing, starting a crash diet. There isn't a smooth or peaceful transition because the elements aren't in integrated balance in our lives. We move abruptly from one pole to the other and, like sitting high on the teeter-totter, it feels out of control and maybe a little scary.

Building balance into our lives is something our parents may have encouraged us to do when we were young. They tried to provide balanced meals and may have coaxed us to spend some time with friends and some alone. In school, extracurricular activities supplemented curricular activities as a balance. The colleges, guidance counselors told us, were looking for well-rounded applicants.

Somewhere along the way the caution to balance seemed to shift, and we noticed that while balance was taught, imbalance was often rewarded. The most highly sought after and touted students often had a single focus and skill, sometimes academics or more often athletics. All work and no play might make Jill or Jack dull, but it couldn't help but make an impression at promotion time. Many of our generation grew up with parents, particularly fathers, who seemed to have to deny parts of themselves—to live out of balance—in order to make a go of it at their jobs. Work weighed down one end of their teeter-totters.

The key aspects of our lives that we seek to balance over time form a network like a spider web, where all the delicate strands are woven together to create an integrated whole. And what are the strands? Work, leisure and fun; friends and family; community; caring for our physical, mental and spiritual well-being; balancing the past, present and future. They all come into play.

Balance entails wholeness and symmetry. Balance occurs when parts are in equilibrium: each is given some attention and none is used to the point of depletion. Balance is some challenge!

We write of balance because for us it is a fundamental building block in crafting satisfying and effective lives. When we ignore an important part of ourselves for too long, we not only get out of sorts but our effectiveness declines, even in that particular area that has been the focus of our time and attention. We write of balance to heighten awareness of the mixed messages we receive in our families, schools, churches and workplaces about the importance of different elements of our lives.

In *Lives Without Balance*, Steven Carter and Julia Sokol note that when we don't have balance we are, at least implicitly, putting some parts of our lives on hold. We feel called to balance and wholeness; we want to take those parts of life off hold. Wanna be my partner on the teeter-totter?

Tis a gift to be simple,
Tis a gift to be free.

A Shaker Hymn

Our new kitten arrived on a day that had been terrible for both of us. We weren't even sure we wanted to keep him, even though he was a gift. Being responsible for another living thing just seemed too taxing at that time in our lives.

But what a gift he has been, showing us the joy of simplicity. He lives purely in the moment, fully enjoying what he is doing as he is doing it. And he has the best of times with simple, readily available things such as string and crumpled paper. Most of the time he seems to do what he wants to do, probably what brings him fulfillment as a cat.

As we took delight in him, we realized that we too could marvel in the simple and readily available, that we could be joyous with what is near at hand—friendships, family, walks, the first robin of spring, the morning after a big snowfall, hearty soup, reading by the fire.

It is a gift to be simple because simplicity is one of the foundations of true freedom and joy.

Today I will take delight in something that
is simple and near at hand.

---

*We worship our work; we work at our play;
and we play at our worship.*

Charles Swindoll

A life of busyness can pull us so far off course, can so disorient us, that we approach elemental facets of our lives in ways that prevent us from getting the intended benefits.

Through our work, we seek the self-esteem that comes from being productive, making a contribution to society and earning a living. When we make our work all-important, we end up putting far too much of our time and energy—ourselves—into it, and our lives become distorted.

When we make our play work by taking it so seriously, having to have exactly the right equipment and making it another forum for competition, the same thing happens. We lose the beneficial effects of play—camaraderie, exercise, a change of pace, stress release, *fun*!

Worship is a time to set aside other pursuits, a time to forget both work and play even though worship is both serious and joyful. It is first a time of taking in, of concentrating on one's relationship with God and connectedness to all life, seen and unseen. Then it is a time of focusing outward, of preparing to serve and to give. Worship is a time when something bigger than yourself is the center of attention.

But some people bring work and social agendas to worship. They need to attend the "right" place of worship and be seen among the "right" people. Worship becomes a way to extend work and play.

A key to thriving in life is to live in the present moment, enjoying what life offers now because now is really the only time we have. To flourish and thrive, we attend to what is before us at any given moment.

*I will work during my work, play during my play,
and worship during my worship.*

Live . . . Be you . . . Enjoy . . . Love . . .

Wayne Dyer

Live! Don't just be alive, live! Savor each precious day and life itself. Awake at sunrise. Be awed by vast skies teeming with stars and by the intricacies of a dragonfly's wing. Pulse with the life of the city. Be renewed in your special place of peace.

Be you! Express your specialness. Rejoice in being you. Let your music play. Know and share your gifts. Make a contribution. Appreciate yourself. Find a place where you can be you and find people who encourage you.

Enjoy! Enjoy the everyday pleasure life gives—friends, tasty food, stars, kittens, a roaring fire, a walk in the woods, a good book, satisfying work, loved ones. Relish all the good things the earth provides for our sustenance.

Love! Love your family and your neighbor. Respect the life of and care for other creatures. Practice and spread love. Cherish the earth as sustainer of all life. Love your God. And don't forget to love yourself.

What a prescription for a great day! What a formula for a good life!

Today I will live fully, enjoy life,
be myself and express love.

To live plainly is to distinguish between . . .
what you desire and what is in your best interest.

M.M. Kirsch

In the hustle and bustle of daily life, it is a challenge even to be aware of—let alone act on—our own best interests. What do you regard as being in your own best interests? What practices and commitments will serve you and yours best in the long run?

Your own well-being might be best served by practices such as

- Sustaining a reasonable balance between work and the other facets of your life
- Eating nutritious foods
- Exercising regularly
- Nurturing your loved ones and friendships
- Taking time to serve others
- Creating work that allows you to express yourself and contribute to others
- Regularly acknowledging and developing your spiritual connections
- Moderation in material things

We may desire other things—more sleep instead of exercise or prayer, extra dessert, another piece of jewelry or computer equipment, finishing a pressing project at the office rather than connecting with our spiritual community. Occasionally that is okay; life is not going to whirl off its moorings if our desires take over from time to time. But creating congruence between our desires and our best interests is optimal in the long run.

Today I will act on my own
best interests.

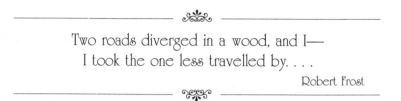

Two roads diverged in a wood, and I—
I took the one less travelled by. . . .

Robert Frost

Perhaps you too are one who took the road less traveled, while many of the rest of us chose the more-traveled route and now yearn to explore the other fork.

Where would your road less traveled lead?

- Would it be a path toward more peace and balance, less stress and drudgery?
- Would it involve realigning your life so you could have more time and energy to spend with family or working on important causes?
- Would it be a journey of sharing some of what you have with someone who has less?
- Would it allow time away from customary responsibilities to pursue learning or to raise a child?
- Would it allow you to experience parts of yourself that have been hidden or downplayed for many years?
- Would the destination be unknown, becoming clear only as your pathway unfolded?

In Frost's poem, taking the road less traveled made "all the difference." Imagine the difference a new route could make now in your life—expressing long-dormant values, growing and knowing yourself in ways that simply would not have happened on the other fork.

This week I will spend some time on a less-traveled road that I yearn to travel more.

---

*If we will take the good we find asking no
questions we shall have heaping measures.
The great gifts are not got by analysis.*

Ralph Waldo Emerson

Asking questions is often a good thing to do. Failing to ask the right questions can get us into trouble when we do things such as change jobs, sign a contract, buy a house or plan a trip to a place we have never been. Asking questions is a way of knowing that calls on us to be analytical and critical, to step back and detach from life a bit.

I have lived much of my life presuming that good would come from analysis, that the answers to life's pressing questions would be found in the next book, the right philosophy, the emerging model. Much of my life, particularly my professional life, is still focused on using my analytical mind to achieve the results I seek.

But all ways of knowing have arenas where they are more—and less—fruitfully used. In recent years I have begun to experience the limitations of relying so heavily on analysis. The good, the pleasure and the joy found in friendships, in love and in spiritual connections often come without the mediator of analysis. They come much more directly as raw experience. In those few times, for example, when I believe I have experienced God, analysis has had no role.

Those of us schooled in the West tend to rely heavily on the mind and to value its fruits more highly than other ways of knowing. In doing so, we may cut ourselves off from much of the richness life has to offer.

*Today I will accept the good I receive
without questioning it.*

For the measure you give will be the
measure you get back.

Luke 6:38

Many religious and philosophical traditions have a statement like the Golden Rule that focuses us on the active part we play in creating the conditions in which we live. A recent experience brought this home to me. My wife and I are both very trusting people who move through life taking people at their word. Most of the time this works out just fine; occasionally we get into a situation we later regret.

Recently we applied to refinance our house. In the initial interview the mortgage banker warned me that the process could be obtrusive. Even with that warning, here's what happened: as they asked for more and more information and acted as though they did not trust the information we first gave them, I felt they didn't trust us.

Then an interesting and scary thing happened—I began to distrust them. Although they had taken nearly $1,000 from us and we had been living in and making payments on the house for over five years, they hinted that we would not be approved for a new mortgage. I began to envision a huge scam where they would reject our application yet keep our money. My usually trusting self had vanished quickly in the face of apparent distrust.

That experience made me appreciate how I usually am with others and the way they usually are with me. It also made me aware of how quickly a situation can change and how quickly mistrust can be created. The positive qualities we seek are fragile and require regular attention to preserve.

I will be with others the way I want
others to be with me.

---

*My conviction is that simplicity is related
essentially to integrity, that the simple life is
the integrated life with all of the
essentials included. . . .*

Dan West

As humans we are called to wholeness and balance, challenged
to bring all the parts of our lives together. And what a challenge it
is when we are pushed and pulled in so many directions, bom-
barded with countless invitations to give up our focus and balance
and to put off our integrity until another day or another year. Living
in balance is a daily effort for all, the work of a lifetime for many.

Wholeness entails integrating our physical, emotional, intellectual, social and spiritual needs. When I reach my highest frustration
level and yearn for relief, it is usually when one part of my life (typically work) has taken over and thrown the other parts out of balance. It feels like being on one side of a playground seesaw when
most of the weight is on the other side—the only options that seem
possible are crashing to the ground or staying stuck up in the air.

It is during those times that I especially feel the call to balance
and to integrate all the parts of my life, to give work, family, friends,
community and myself an appropriate share of time, resources and
energy. When I am high in the air on the weightless end of the seesaw, achieving integration and simplicity seems an enormous task,
another impossible thing to add to my "to do" list. But when simplicity comes and the pieces fit together better, there is peace,
power and synergy.

*I claim wholeness and balance
as my calling.*

Inaction may be the highest form of action.

Jerry Brown

"I'm too busy." "I can't do that right now." "If only I had an hour to myself." Whether student or executive, mother or grandfather, there is always something to do. Often the challenge is in not doing something rather than in doing it.

When was the last time you sat by a pond, walked through a new neighborhood, listened to the sounds in your backyard? When we do nothing, time almost always does something magical. It is time when our minds are free to roam, to fasten on new ideas, new solutions to problems, new hope. It is time when we notice beauty, kindness, the goodness in our world.

Inaction renews energy, commitment and focus. Inaction saves us from angry response, exhaustion and hopelessness. It is necessary to rest so that we may begin anew, afresh.

*When I am forced by circumstances into a
period of inaction—waiting in the dentist's office,
in traffic, or between appointments—I will make
the most of the opportunity for renewal.*

I no longer ask the young man's question:
How far will I go? My questions are now those of
the mature person: When it is over, what
will my life have been about?

Harold Kushner

Even though I wouldn't always classify myself as a mature person, I no longer ask how far I will go and I'm pretty sure my life is not about recognition or making lots of money. It's not that I would refuse fame or fortune if it had been legitimately acquired. I just no longer spend any effort trying to make those things happen.

What life is about now is trying to focus on those few things that are really important to me. To be a good friend and a good parent. To be better every day at the professional pursuit I have chosen. To give my time and talents to my community so that it is a little better for my having given them. To love wholeheartedly those persons I have chosen to love. To actively respect creation.

I am intentional about what my life
will have meant when it is over.

*The still mind of the sage is a mirror
of heaven and earth.*

Chuang Tzu

There are a million thoughts that swirl unbidden in my mind at any given moment in the day. When I am at work, talking with a friend or child, gardening, taking a bath, the background buzz is always operative. Sometimes I am surprised that I have worked out a solution to a conflict without "having thought about it." Of course, I did think about it, I just wasn't conscious of having considered that particular conflict.

More often, though, I am annoyed by the incessant mutterings of my mind. "Will you shut up?" I ask it when I am exhausted. When I am afraid, I find that my fitful sleep just barely interrupts the cacophony of those reproachful conversants in my brain.

It takes practice to still the mind, practice as repetitive and intentional as an athlete's. I have begun to practice in order to slow myself down, to find what my mind really wants to say to me. I cannot tell you what happens in that practice except that my mind is often open, receptive, willing rather than willful. And when my mind is in this state my body relaxes too. The aftereffects seem to be a more peaceful approach to life itself.

*What a simple gift a still mind is,
and what a precious one.*

---

*Angels can fly because they take
themselves lightly.*

G.K. Chesterton

It is very important to be silly. Not to be silly in any particular way, but to have your own pockets of silliness. My husband and son create word sillies. When discussing the fertilization of figs by certain species of wasps, my husband responds, "Some people are very upset about the practice of dissecting these figs." I know some silly is coming. At almost the same moment father and son explode with, "They are known as the anti-FIG-isection league." Both of them laugh in appreciation of their mind reading as well as their humor.

My silliness tends to be nonverbal. I make faces at children in the supermarket or in the back of station wagons. I tickle my husband or chase him around the backyard for no reason other than that I feel like it. I send him and others silly cards.

Life is so serious. Real problems of interaction between different peoples, disrespectful interaction with our earth, and production and consumption of so many minimally differentiated products require our attention and careful consideration. If we take our lives seriously and ourselves lightly we may proceed gently and with good humor toward resolutions and caring.

*When I have not been silly for a long time,
life loses some of its sweetness.*

A system built round a purpose is dead before it
is born. Purpose unfolds and reflects the means.

Mary Parker Follett

So many organizations concentrate on writing a mission statement that describes who they are and what they wish to stand for
in their market and in the world. The mission statement becomes
the foundation for strategic planning, the blueprint for carrying out
their mission.

It is much less common for an individual to create a personal
mission statement, although I think it is a good idea. A strategic plan
is most commonly plotted by individuals in journals, as part of self-
enrichment workshops or as professional goals.

Having a purpose isn't bad. Knowing what form we want our life
to take is important. Besides, how can we know if we have suc-
ceeded if we don't have a definition of success? What is often coun-
terproductive about a system is that its purpose is not necessarily
examined on an ongoing basis.

A business whose purpose is to build the best widget in the
world and sell it at the lowest price will go bankrupt if the need for
widgets evaporates. In a more personal system, a family whose purpose is to support each other at any cost may not remain intact if
some members abuse others.

In starting something, or focusing on something, we need to
know what our purpose is. In growing something, including ourselves, we want to pay attention to the unfolding purpose and how
it changes.

*I am not the same person I was a year ago,
nor is my purpose the same.*

———————————— ✻ ————————————

In order to be utterly happy the only thing
necessary is to refrain from comparing this moment
with other moments in the past, which I often
did not fully enjoy because I was comparing
them with other moments of the future.

André Gide

———————————— ✻ ————————————

Last evening I spent a few hours with old friends. We laughed
a lot, we ate a fair amount and we made plans for an activity that
would bring us together on an irregular basis. The evening was
informal, inexpensive (we all chipped in) and productive. I was
aware of my own contentment.

Today I am anxious, unable to concentrate and self-blaming.
What happened? I believe the anxiety is about a decision made in
the past that affects my future but not my today. The restlessness
has to do with something that will happen later this week about
which I am fearful. I can do nothing about either the past decision
or the future events.

My friends are still my friends in this moment. My life is secure
in this moment. Yet my meditation is fragmented. My frightened
feelings are intense. I berate myself for having made an expedient
rather than a long-term choice. Enough.

A squirrel cocks his tiny ears as he looks through the skylight at
me.

*Even when I cannot control my propensity for
comparing this moment to others, I can stop
to appreciate something in the now.*

⚜

When a lion kills and devours its prey it may
not be a pretty sight, but the lion isn't
bad for doing what is natural for lions to do.

David Reynolds

⚜

What is natural for humans? Is it natural for us to compete and acquire, to disregard the needs of other humans and other creatures, to disregard the earth's need to regenerate? Or is it natural for humans to want to live in harmony with other humans and their environment?

Perhaps it is natural for us to want all of these things at various times in our lives. Youth may spend its energy on competition, whereas age seeks harmony with all things. This is undoubtedly an oversimplification, but it contains some truth. Olympians are almost exclusively young, as are boundlessly energetic beginning lawyers and doctors. Corporate executives and entrepreneurs compete well into their 60s and beyond, but they also may dote on families and give time and money generously to environmental or social welfare programs. We construct nests in our youth and divest ourselves of them in old age.

The gift of life creates so much choice, and the course of life demands that we make choices. As we learn more about the dangers to our bodies of constant stress, drug abuse and high-fat diets, and the dangers to our environment of overharvesting, we may naturally change our wants to fit with the perceived wants of the earth.

In all things,
ultimate balance is natural.

---✿---

If I am content with what I have,
I can live simply and enjoy both prosperity
and free time.

John Heider

---✿---

Sometimes being content with what we have seems easy. On a bright fall morning or a gentle spring afternoon, when just being outdoors is enough to bring joy to our hearts, contentment is as natural as breathing. Lovemaking, bread baking and singing are other personal favorites for creating a sense of all being right with the world. Of these, only bread baking costs anything at all.

There are other times, however, when our ability to live simply is challenged. Professional deadlines, family stress, even the temporary "needs" created by advertising, can make pressure to earn more and do more the order of the day. Appreciating what we already have, even if that is very little in the great scheme of American consumerism, can seem pretty simplistic.

Funny how simple and simplistic have such different connotations. Simple is almost always good. Simplistic is—well, none of us would like to be described that way. But almost anything we are usually content with—a pet, time to do our favorite thing, a nap—is quite simple. It is when we do not have those contentments that our lives seem overwhelming and complex.

I want to spend ten minutes today appreciating
something about my life that already exists,
something that makes me content.

❦

Power comes through cooperation,
independence through service, and a greater
self through selflessness.

John Heider

❦

This sounds good, but is it really true? Is it one of those plati-
tudes that makes the author sound like he lives on some higher
plane than the rest of us? Hmm. What examples of power, independence or selflessness can you think of in your own life?

I feel most powerful when I am doing good work, writing or
speaking to prospective clients about their needs. Writing, like
painting or sewing or designing, is solitary work. I am cooperating,
though, with my inner longing to communicate thoughts with others. When I am interviewing clients or just talking with them, I am
cooperating by acknowledging their perceptions and attempting to
find whether I can fit my talents with their needs.

Independence does not mean that I can do everything by myself.
What good are our gifts if they are not given in service to some
greater good, a better trash bag, a simpler set of instructions?

And finally, developing the self does not mean giving my self
away. That isn't selflessness, it is self-destruction. But when I am
there for someone, or when I can do something for someone just
because I want to and not because it will do me any good, I build
confidence in and shape my self.

Perhaps what may have sounded at first like empty words really
has some meaning for us all. Power, independence and self exer-
cised in the world with respect for others enhances both the world
and ourselves.

Sometimes I am tempted to dismiss thoughts
I do not think I can live up to.

I feel I am like a hierarchy, and perhaps
I am one. I am my own chief interest because to me,
I am life. My curiosity, delight, pain tell
me about life itself.

Florida Scott-Maxwell

While it is a lesson of life to learn that the self is not the center of all life, it is also a lesson to learn to value what we learn by paying attention to our selves. Too much attention to my self leaves little time or willingness to explore and interpret the beauty and the cruelty around me. Too little attention to self leaves me unable to replenish and to adjust to the world. Self-love is healthy, even necessary. Self-absorption is limiting; little else can be taken in. But oh, the balancing act.

Our feelings can be the basis for empathizing with another's feelings. Our achievement can be a source of celebration of another's achievement. But our disappointments and fears can limit the ability to accept another or to accept life as it is.

Eastern philosophies suggest observing our feelings without making them our whole reality. Our fear or anger can be very real, and yet not all of reality. In observing feelings rather than acting on them right away, sometimes the feeling or the situation changes, allowing more than the self into the picture. When we are not blown about by the power of our feelings, we notice our own self, but we do not make the self the only thing worth noticing.

Balance involves practice. Its achievement
is delicate and momentary.

Our constant problem is how to live with
people and remain free, how to live with things
and remain independent.

Abraham Joshua Heschel

When other people—parents, spouse, friends, children—are our reasons to live a certain way, we are not truly free. This does not mean that we should not choose to marry or commit to a relationship, to have children, to care for aging parents. The consequences of these choices may restrict our other choices, but this restriction of our freedom is very different from using others as an excuse to live in ways that cause us to feel resentment and hostility toward them.

Living with things allows both comfort and liability. At a certain level homes, cars, clothing and discretionary income give us freedom to enjoy life. But when our entire lives are spent generating the means to support a lifestyle, there is more and more restriction on our independence.

Freedom is precious. It allows us to truly enjoy the people we love. Independence from possessions permits the detachment to judge what is most important to each of us and to focus our life purpose on that importance.

In the best relationships I am free to be myself.
Owning and caring for only those things that
permit my greatest creativity keep me
independent from them.

---

*Every day we do things, we are things,
that have to do with peace. If we are aware of
our lifestyle, our way of consuming, of looking
at things, we will know how to make peace
right in the moment we are alive,
the present moment.*

Thich Nhat Hanh

Being and doing. Sipping a hot drink on a cold morning, noticing the birds, their sounds and movement, the colors and light of a new spring day. How often do we slow down enough to hear and see the beauty of life around us, to just be? Perhaps you might chide that this is a luxury of the single person or the unemployed. But it is in our awareness that we feel and sense peacefulness, not in our activity, or lack of activity.

When our breathing slows and all of our senses take in the messages of the natural world, we can grasp its integrity. Once grasped, it is important to protect the natural world from the destruction of mindless consuming, from unkindness to creatures other than our human sisters and brothers and from our own disregard of those sisters and brothers in our hurry to get something or somewhere.

*Morning, teach my heart the bird song,
the wind rustle, the light playing on waves and
windowsills. Teach me peace.*

---

*Consciousness is always open to many
possibilities because it involves play.
It is always an adventure.*

Julian Jaynes

Walking along the river each morning, I look for the familiar. I expect the couple who walk their three large dogs and the man who throws tennis balls to his puppy in the same place on my route. I smell the sewage treatment vapors coming through a vent in a cement box. I say "good morning" to many of the same folks.

Each day there is a surprise of some kind. Today it was the crane coming toward me along the road, swinging a menacing metal ball and hook at the end of its very long arm. Several weeks ago it was the motor sailor anchored offshore that had arrived during the night. New wildflowers spring up beside the path. New faces travel the same route. The river changes color. A sudden rainstorm soaks me to the skin.

If I am worried about something that is happening in my world, I am not as open to the outside adventures along my walk. If I am absorbed by my inner conversation, I am not as aware of the wrecking ball or the intense purple blossoms. To let go of these worries, even for the hour it takes to walk across two bridges, is to be conscious of the beauty and complexity of life, to play among the beetles and the fish and the in-line skaters.

*Being conscious may mean being playful,
seeking adventure, expecting
the unexpected.*

--------------------------------- ❧ ---------------------------------

Wow! Those chickadees are just moving constantly.
How could you live life like that?

Bradley Demarest

--------------------------------- ❧ ---------------------------------

The chickadees are moving constantly because it is about 5° above zero as we watch them gathering seeds and suet, their fuel against the cold. It is part of their nature, their "chickadeeness," to flit about.

The chickadees have a good reason for moving constantly, but do we?

On vacation in Hawaii we found ourselves moving about a lot, despite the fact that the preceding months had been exceedingly busy and we needed the vacation to rejuvenate. We came all this way, we reasoned, and we might never come again, so we should see everything we could—right? We ended up moving constantly like the chickadees.

True, survival in our world requires much movement and busy involvement—so much that movement has become ingrained in us. We stay in motion even during those times when we don't need to be, when it would be in our best interests not to be.

The Biblical incantation "Be still and know . . ." reflects the wisdom that we need stillness to know ourselves and to know the sacred.

*I will find ten minutes of stillness
for myself each day.*

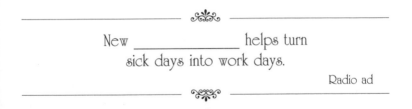

New _____ helps turn
sick days into work days.

Radio ad

In this ad the announcer discovers two children who are absent from school because their mother is ill and can't take them. After taking the advertiser's product she is well enough to drive them to school. The announcer concludes triumphantly, "New _____ helps turn sick days into work days."

Great, I thought. Just what we need—another way to devote even more time to work. We are allowed sick days to be sick, but apparently we shouldn't use them. We should take pills instead. Perhaps next we will develop a medicine so we won't need to use our vacation time either. I can hear it now: "New _____ helps turn vacation days into work days." What madness!

While appropriate use of medication can be part of maintaining our health, using drugs to help us carry out our normal routines when we really need to be resting seems harmful and short-sighted, not restorative. Despite what others might expect, we should not tough it out and turn sick days into anything but days to be sick.

*I will allow time for healing and
restoration when I need to.*

Enjoy your ice cream while
it is on your plate.

Thornton Wilder

While birding with two friends one spring morning, I noticed a tree in front of us that held several interesting birds. Yet it was the season of migration, so we might expect to do even better. "Should we stay here or move down the path?" one of us asked. Sure that the next best bird was just around the bend in the trail, we moved ahead.

Although the path ahead was pretty, it did not reveal any new birds. We didn't eat the ice cream on our plates—it melted.

Enjoying the present moment is particularly challenging for those of us whose attention naturally tends to travel into the future. We are convinced that the next plate of ice cream will be bigger or tastier or somehow more satisfying than the one we have now.

Although it is trite to say that the present moment is all we have, I will say it because it is true.

I will enjoy the ice cream on my plate
and *look forward to the next time*
I expect to relish it.

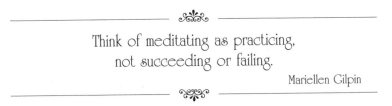

Think of meditating as practicing,
not succeeding or failing.

Mariellen Gilpin

Many religious and spiritual traditions hold meditation as a way to get in touch with the Divine in and outside of ourselves. In recent years, meditation has been touted as a way to cure, or at least relieve the symptoms of, disease. So many good things from such a simple practice! And yet I find it maddeningly difficult to do.

Meditation is difficult for all the obvious reasons. It is hard to find time. It is hard to slow the mind. It is hard to sit/lie/stand still. All of these speak to the difficulty I find in making meditation a habit. When I meditate regularly enough for days or even weeks to see the internal benefits (lowered stress levels, a calmness not characteristic of my personality and better sleep), I wonder why I don't do it every day. Then, for reasons that seem important at the time, I let the practice slip away.

In this year, in this second half of my life, in this frame of mind, I claim meditation as something I will practice, not succeed at. On the days when quieting my mind is impossible, or on the days when I am rushed and making excuses for not meditating, I will try to remember that this is a skill I am practicing. Perhaps some day in the future will find me having made meditation a habit I practice regularly.

Today I will practice meditation,
just as I practice other skills I want to improve.

Our destination is never a place, but rather
a new way of looking at things.

Henry Miller

Actually one of my desired destinations is a place. It is in the woods, near water, has abundant birds and wildlife and is peaceful. Although I don't know where it is, I can see it clearly.

When I get there, I will not think I have arrived. I will still be on the journey, still in process, still baking.

How will I look at things differently then? I don't know for sure. I imagine I will have what we call "perspective." Things that were once important will be less so. Little, seemingly insignificant things—next spring's bud waiting on a branch throughout the entire winter, a newly arrived bird, the first ice of autumn on a puddle— may be the highlight of the day.

Are there new ways of looking at things that I need to adopt now to move toward that perspective? How might I be blocking my own growth, impeding my own journey? Maybe it is by thinking of my destination instead of my journey.

I delight in the journey.

A person without a sense of humor is like
a wagon without springs—jolted by
every pebble in the road.

Henry Ward Beecher

Humor helps us manage the pebbles, rocks, boulders and pot-holes on life's road. It makes our encounters with these bumps smoother. Like the springs of the wagon, laughter can buffer us and make the journey more enjoyable.

Humor is very important in my work and life. I look for it, use it and try to create it with others. It helps me laugh at myself and, I hope, with others. Although my work is often serious, if I couldn't laugh and have fun while doing it, I would stop.

Laughing, especially at ourselves during a particularly difficult moment, can relieve the tension and be a reminder not to take our-selves so seriously. It's not that there aren't serious problems in our lives and the world—there most certainly are—but laughter can help keep things in perspective.

Smile, chuckle, grin, giggle,
guffaw, LAUGH!

Consciously be grateful for the good in
your life. . . . Be thankful for little things,
big things, everything.

John-Roger and Peter McWilliams

What am I thankful for today?

For love,
for choices,
for family,
for opportunities to serve,
for cats,
for community,
for celebrations,
for waterfalls,
for sunshine,
for forgiveness,
for birds,
for spring,
for friends,
for favorite foods,
for grace,
for gratitude.

I am grateful for so many things.
I raise my voice in thanksgiving.

*Ordinary people can and do inspire others
into healthier, more mature choices
and behaviors.*

Marsha Sinetar

A friend of mine plans to begin a women's leadership discussion group that will meet once a week for the next six months. She has asked me to join. Although I am excited about it, I wonder what 10 or 12 ordinary women can do about affecting the kind of leadership we have witnessed and/or practiced.

I remember clearly a high school teacher who inspired my keen interest in current events, which led to my acceptance at a fine women's college.

Another instructor in graduate school inspired careful research into women's ministry.

My husband inspires tolerance of all creatures and fierce commitment to those he loves.

My daughter inspires single-mindedness, focus and adherence to a cause.

Of course a group of friends and new acquaintances will inspire new ways to think about leadership. I have been led by just such ordinary groups and individuals all my life!

*Mystics can emerge from the
most ordinary situations.*

But now—now—she was filled with the
realization that her inner life was in harmony with
the world outside. She relaxed the tight fibers
of her being which she had unwittingly held
rigid during the cold gray months.

Mary Fahy

Sometimes when I am the passenger (or even the driver) on a long road trip in the car, I leave my body and go to other places and have other conversations in my head. I am hardly ever aware of doing it until my husband asks if I am okay. It is a response to boredom, I suppose. Too many corn fields, too many pine forests or just too much sitting probably triggers these flights.

Sometimes my body seems to go away for days or weeks at a time. It shuts down much the way I imagine a tree does in the winter. I am hardly ever aware of it until it is over and I feel my body again. The shutting down is almost always in response to fear. Under the prolonged stress of fear I will simply go away physically to protect myself from the punishing winter of a job loss or an abusive relationship.

When my husband brings my attention back to the front seat of our car, and the present reality of a river valley or a herd of sheep outside its windows, I am amused by the "otherness" of my imagination. When my body returns after weeks of fearful tightness, I am grateful for both its ability to protect itself and its ability to shut down. I am frightened, though, in both cases at how easily I lose touch with my whole self and the self's needs.

I will try to be aware of all the parts
of myself—body, mind, spirit—when I am peaceful
and when I am not.

———————————— ⚜ ————————————

- Be reactive; doubt yourself and blame others.
  - Work without any clear end in mind.
    - Do the urgent thing first.
      - Think win/lose.
    - Seek first to be understood.
    - If you can't win, compromise.
  - Fear change and put off improvement.

John Covey

———————————— ⚜ ————————————

Stephen Covey's brother coined the above Seven Habits of Ineffective People to jolt readers and clients into an awareness of the destructiveness of many common business and relationship practices. These habits are frequently mine.

- So often I doubt my willingness to let go of the complexity of my life even though I have long since seen the liabilities of complexity.
- Most days my goal is clouded even though I say I know what I want.
- How many urgent things have I done already today without making room for the truly significant?
- There is always at least one person with whom I am butting heads. When I stop butting one head, another presents itself.
- Listening is not one of my highly developed skills. Explaining is.
- If I can't win, I roll over and play dead. Is this better than compromise?
- For most of what I expect to have of this life, I have prepared for the "big event." Even after quasi-big events, I am still getting ready.

Today I can shape my present to fit my goals.

---⚜---

*Which one of us listens to the hymn of the
brook when the tempest speaks?*

Kahlil Gibran

---⚜---

So many times since I began to see the wisdom of simplifying my life I have caught myself listening to the tempests of the moment and disregarding the music of the ever-flowing brooks. Just this week I raced home from work only to race off to the grocery store, to race home to fix dinner, to race through dinner to get ready for a daughter's birthday party, to race through that so I could go to bed at a decent hour. I couldn't enjoy the pleasures of any of those experiences because of the tempest of too much to do.

Even when I have a moment to rest I fill it with reading and talking and rarely with appreciation of the music of the world around me or the internal music of my soul. On the rare occasions when I find myself without a book or work to do, I fight the silence and the space by searching for something to fill it. A magazine. A phone call. A conversation.

Of course there are real tempests in life, tempests that call for our undivided attention. Friends or children are sick or in trouble. Parents need us, and we need them. An economic crisis causes personal trauma. But so much of what we call a tempest is simply manufactured busyness overlaying the music of life underneath it.

*Today I will listen for the hymns of
the quiet things in my life.*

—————————————————— ⟡ ——————————————————

Don't compromise yourself.
You're all you've got.

Janis Joplin

—————————————————— ⟡ ——————————————————

A recent dinner table conversation revolved around the question: "Why do people stay in destructive relationships?" All of us
knew someone who was attached to someone who was mean,
dependent or in some way detrimental to the well-being of the
other and to the relationship. Why couldn't they see it? And if they
could, why did they stay there?

Having been in a few not-so-great relationships myself, I suggested that staying past one's realization of dis-ease involved low
self-esteem. This is no new revelation. I'm no psychological genius.
But I know that I was an adult (chronologically) for many years
before I understood, accepted and even liked myself. Once I got to
this place I no longer wanted to be with other people who did not
like or accept me the way I was.

This is an aspect of simplicity that is impossible to teach. One
must learn it from the inside out. We are, ultimately, all we've got.
If we spend time and energy compromising our own needs, our
own dreams, our own soul to be with someone else, we waste the
uniqueness of who we are. Our soul may not seem like much if we
do not like ourselves, but it is everything.

Each individual gifts another with relationship.
Consider the receiver carefully.

Learn to say "No"; it will be of more use to
you than to be able to read Latin.

Charles Haddon Spurgeon

Long before I learned to read Latin, I learned to say "no." My children each went through a period of a year or so when they answered "no" to almost every question. The pediatric guru of my young adulthood defined this period as "the terrible twos." It was a period when they and I tested new boundaries between ourselves and others.

Learning to live more simply isn't unlike the terrible twos. It is a time of learning about boundaries between ourselves and the environment and our interaction with it, and also about boundaries between people and how we want to define our relationships with them.

Living simply requires saying "no" to a steady stream of stimulation from our culture: "no" to media invitations to consume; "no" to requests for my participation in all kinds of worthy and not so worthy endeavors; "no" to working too hard and long at my profession even when it is satisfying; and "no" to more noise. The knee-jerk "no" is essential to getting the ball rolling. Only after I know I can say "no" do I really feel like I have that choice. As for the two-year-old, there is invaluable learning in establishing new and more suitable boundaries in our lives. I have long since forgotten most of the Cicero I read. But I can say "no" and I will.

*Saying "no" is a positive choice that leads me
to more freedom and simplicity.*

────────────────── ✤ ──────────────────

Service never asks you to do what you cannot do,
but only what you most truly can do.

J. Ruth Gendler

────────────────── ✤ ──────────────────

Reading one of those long feel-good pieces in the Sunday news-paper (why is it that in-depth reporting or essays seem more and more to be restricted to the Sunday paper?), I became aware of my current inactivity as a volunteer.

The journalist wrote of a man raised in poverty, with a restricting physical condition, who gave hours of his work week to teach children table manners and simple banking as well as more theoretical subjects such as self-esteem.

I realized in reading this that I had been "out of service" for several years. Oh, I write for some professional publications as a volunteer, but I haven't given time on a regular basis to any organization or group of people who could use an extra pair of hands, a loaf of bread or a telephone voice. There are so many things I know that I take for granted because I have had the privilege of money and education. I want to move outside my normal responsibilities and give.

The act of giving, of serving others, is a simple
gift to both the giver and the receiver.

---— ❧ ——---

Why are we here? . . . We're here to feel
the joy of life pulsing in us now.

Joyce Carol Oates

---— ❧ ——---

I had just introduced the mental technique of "staying in the present" during a stress-management workshop when a man approached me and said, "I guess that means I should stop trying to read journal articles while I'm playing with my child." "I'd say you're right about that," I responded, wondering how he could do those two things at once.

Enjoying the moment—sometimes even being aware of it—has been one of the biggest challenges for me. Instead of experiencing now, I am frequently busy anticipating the next event or pondering one that has passed.

It is not hard for me to stay focused on the present when I am caught up in something that is especially captivating to me, such as watching birds or taking pictures. But it is difficult when the matters at hand are less interesting. (Maybe the lesson is to spend more time with birds and cameras!)

There isn't much in our culture (besides advertising and self-help books) that encourages us to enjoy life now. We are encouraged to prepare for, plan for and save for the future. All these are prudent things to do, but if we are always preparing for what is to come we miss what is happening now.

I can *feel the joy of life
in this moment.*

Don't forget to live!

Johann W. Goethe

Right now this is advice I need to heed. It is a holiday season, with extra activities and events added to my typical spring busyness. Today there were two telephone lines ringing at the same time while I was answering the front door to sign for a piece of overnight mail. That sure didn't feel simple and peaceful!

Right now it seems like there is a lot of preparation for living rather than simply living. I dream of next summer's canoe trip, plans for an August wedding and the business trip to Singapore in July. One son is preparing to go to Africa and the other is hopeful of finding summer work out of state. I will be leaving for Chicago at 4:00 a.m. on Tuesday, returning on Thursday, then heading to Los Angeles for an all-day workshop on Sunday.

Right now it's not that I have forgotten to live, it's just that I am so busy getting ready to live that I don't have time to live in the moment. I am not the only one doing this. After all, the plane to L.A. on Saturday night won't be empty.

I need help balancing living with
preparing and remembering.

⟶ ⟶ ✦ ⟵ ⟵

We all too often become aware of the
importance of inner guidance only when we
have lost touch with it.

Hal Zina Bennett and Susan J. Sparrow

When is the last time someone asked you, "How's your inner life?" This is not a question we often ask or are asked. When we return to work on Monday we ask, "What did you do this weekend?" When we make a decision at work, "inner guidance" does not appear prominently on the checklist of factors to consider. Even in those places, such as churches and seminaries, where you might expect to hear this question, it isn't commonly asked.

In our action-oriented culture, we don't seem to have many opportunities to learn to use and trust our inner wisdom. Often we learn about it, as these authors point out, only by default, only when we have unknowingly violated it.

People know when this happens: when their work no longer makes a contribution, when the flame has gone out in their relationship, when they have wandered so far from their path that they are not even on the map. Then they know something important is missing. Then it is often painful. Sometimes it is too late.

We need to be in touch inwardly long before these points so that we incorporate inner signals into our decisions. We need to learn ways to stay in touch with this source and deliberately tap these ways. We need to teach our children about them as well.

I affirm the importance of innermost guidance,
particularly when it is hard to tap.

————————— ✿ —————————

We carry with us the wonders
we seek without us.

Sir Thomas Browne

————————— ✿ —————————

Sometimes I am seized by uncontrollable laughter. I close my eyes. I make no sound. I shake. Tears escape my squeezed-tight lids. The emotion uses most of the muscles in my body, and when it is spent, so am I.

The source of this hysteria might be a perfectly straightforward sentence in the newspaper, a billboard or a phrase overheard in someone else's conversation. Something about the image or word message sent to my brain throws a switch and I am overtaken by mirth.

This is one of the great free gifts of my life. Perhaps it is inherited. My mother does it too. Her laughter made me laugh as a child, and mine makes my children and my husband laugh too. They hand over the tissues and watch, giggling among themselves until it is over. "What's so funny?" they ask, bewildered. When I tell them, and I usually can't without being seized again by tears and shaking, they almost never think it is as funny as I do.

What a gift to be seized by laughter.
It can appear at any time.

3

Simplicity

O n a typical Saturday during the summer I spend part of my day doing yard work. And when I am cutting grass, pruning shrubs and pulling weeds many of my neighbors are doing the same. As a city dweller, cutting is only half the battle; the other half is packaging the clippings in such a way that the trash haulers will take them away (grass in plastic bags weighing less than 40 pounds and not larger that 33 gallons; prunings not more than three inches in diameter and not more than three feet long, bound with twine in bundles not exceeding 40 pounds).

On a recent Saturday, it suddenly struck me that everything I was doing involved trying to control nature, trying to limit the natural growth processes of spring and summer, and that no matter how hard I tried I was unlikely to triumph in this particular competition. Though I enjoy being in our yard, it was clear to me that spending the bulk of one of my two days off each week in this way was no longer adding to my life. In fact it was keeping me from more important things and something needed to give. I needed to simplify my life, at least in regards to the yard.

Simplify! Oh yes, we have all given ourselves that command at one time or another, whether in regard to our yard, our work, our commuting, our possessions, our spending or our activities. We have too much to do, and less important things seem to conspire to keep us from those that are vital.

Simplicity seems so, well, simple. Cut back; do less; use less; have more time, resources and energy to spend on the significant things; reduce one's impact on the planet; have more available to share with others. The impulse to simplify seems to be harbored deep within us.

Beneath the surface, simplicity may not be quite that simple. Some endorse it for practical reasons, to save money or to not have to devote so much time to yard work. For others, deeply held religious or philosophical beliefs are involved; simplicity is the right way to live, a way to assure that you don't use more than your share of the resources. More recently, living simply has also taken on an ecological rationale. It is a way to help save the planet by reducing our impact on it. For some simplicity is a means; for others it is an end. Alas, simplicity isn't simple.

In the United States, we appear to have a love-hate relationship with simplicity. On the one hand we study and revere those whose lives represent simplicity—Thoreau at Walden, Mother Teresa, Gandhi. On the other hand, our collective actions seem to take us in the other direction. We do more, work more, acquire and consume more, and use more and more resources, in spite of the fact that in some way we

know it is not ultimately in our own best interests.

In their book *Simple Living*, Frank Levering and Wanda Urbanska challenged us to think of simplifying our lives in terms of what we will gain, not what we will give up. Simplification, reducing the excess and the less important so that we can give more attention to the essential and important, can add much. We might gain well-being and peace of mind, resources to spend in ways that have meaning and integrity for us, re-connection to loved ones, the ability to be instead of always having to do. Of course, we will give up some things, but we hope to gain much more.

We write of simplicity because it is a real concern in our own lives and in the lives of our friends as well as our clients. Some are literally being consumed by all they bring on the journey and acquire along the way, not just the material possessions but also responsibilities, obligations and shoulds. Via his title, Alan Durning asks *How Much Is Enough?* We might also ask, "How much is too much?" We write of simplifying because we need to simplify; we have too much in our lives.

*. . . the cost of a thing is the amount of what
I will call life which is required to be exchanged
for it, immediately or in the long run.*

Henry David Thoreau

"Things" are important in our culture. We are expected to spend much of our lives accumulating material possessions. When we are young, everything we own fits in a room or two and can be moved in a small trailer. Later, we need more and more space to hold our things and much larger vehicles to transport them. Many people define themselves by what they possess—house, car, clothes, jewelry, investments, degrees, boats, cabins.

We pay a price for everything. Part of that price is the money we must pay. We also give up a part of our life in work to get that money.

The rest of the price is how much of our life the thing takes up after we have purchased it. Does it have to be maintained? Now that we own it, do we feel obligated to use it? Does it require an alarm system or special insurance? Do we worry about what will happen to it, that a person will hurt it? Do we have to dust or polish it?

Giving up large chunks of life for material things is so automatic that we do not even question it. Often our things complicate our lives rather than enhance them.

*I can examine my life and focus it in ways
that provide balance by remembering that my things
often cost me more than I can afford to give.*

—————————————————— ❧ ——————————————————

Support is the secret to success.
Isolation is the dream killer.

Barbara Sher

—————————————————— ❧ ——————————————————

Even as I write this, I realize that I am trying to pursue my dream while acting on my own. It is difficult for me to ask for help. I am an American male, molded and encouraged to be self-reliant and self-sufficient. I no longer need others to tell me that I should be able to accomplish something on my own; I am my own best reminder.

From my reading and study and observation of others, I know that success in most endeavors requires support and cooperation. This seems particularly true when trying to make personal changes that go against the cultural tide. Then more than ever we need support for our dreams and intentions.

There is a paradox in seeking support. Although accomplishing what we really want often requires a hand from others, we are still responsible for setting the course of our journey. Support provides sustenance, but doesn't relieve us of being in charge.

Such support does not usually come knocking at our door. We have to create it deliberately via colleagues, a support group, spouse, family or special friends. One way to begin to do this is simply to tell others what we are trying to accomplish; we may be surprised at the encouragement we receive.

I can create the support I need to help
make my dream come true.

────────────── ✦ ──────────────

We are all forced to deal with toxic people
in our lives. . . . To offset this, we need
nutritious people. . . .

Richard Leider

────────────── ✦ ──────────────

We recognize our need for nutritious food in our lives. We
need it for health and proper growth. Eating nutritiously helps form
the basis for our ability to live fully. When we don't eat well we
often feel the drain on our energy and vitality.

We may not have thought about the equally important need to
have nutritious people in our lives, people who will nourish and
uphold us in living purposefully, people who (according to Leider)
are truly glad to see us and who don't try to change us.

Sometimes there are toxic people at work or in other areas of our
lives whom we are unable to avoid. Instead, we can take steps to
reduce their effects on us, kind of like applying psychological sun
block. We can also make sure that we are regularly exposed to
nutritious folks, thereby creating an environment where we can
thrive.

*I will acknowledge and celebrate the
people who nourish me.*

❧

The more abundant life is truly more abundant
when we make it available to
those who lack it.

Theodore Hesburgh

Sharing what we have includes all of our resources, not just our money. At various times in the last several years I have watched or taken part in programs that teach people some of the tools to achieve more abundance in their lives. Teaching is better than signing checks precisely because it takes more time.

I have known people who do for others rather than teach, and that takes time too. One man I know participates in an annual paint-a-thon where houses belonging to people who cannot paint them are painted by people who can. This man also goes to one of our state prisons once a year to put on a program for inmates that teaches them about unconditional love and that they are loved unconditionally.

What my friend reports and what I know from my own experience is that the doing and the teaching often nurture him more than those he teaches.

Abundance is contagious.
We get it by giving it away.

If we examine what is behind our desires,
we can usually get what we want without
compromising: love, caring, confidence, respectability,
excitement. Compromising is necessary only
if what we want is in short supply.

Ellen J. Langer

When my thinking is polarized I always compromise. If I can have only one thing and not another, I have to weigh and manipulate to get the most of what I want. Recently I looked at two job opportunities. One allowed me to pursue my own deep interests outside of the job because it was not a full-time commitment, whereas the other allowed me to do full time what I am interested in developing professionally.

I could not do both, so I had to choose. However, if I told myself I would only be happy if I made the right choice for all time, I would have to compromise. Each opportunity offered certain advantages and disadvantages. It was only when I could see (1) that no decision was forever and (2) that the supply of love, caring, confidence, respectability and excitement were not limited to either choice, could I decide for now on the opportunity that seemed to offer the most of what is important to me now.

The supply of good things available to me
is limited only by my willingness to
strive for and accept them.

The life of sensation is the life of greed;
it requires more and more. The life of the spirit
requires less and less; time is ample
and its passage sweet.

Annie Dillard

Is it too harsh to equate sensation with greed? The sensation of the cool water of a stream on warm legs and feet when a summer's sun beats down is a simple pleasure with spiritual elements. Yet the desire for ever more and ever new sensation can lead to a diminishment of the value of creation. Creation gets used up in the quest for new experience.

Stillness allows the appreciation of creation and the awareness of life's natural processes. Oceans roar or whisper without our manipulation. Their sounds and rhythms provide the finest tranquilizer. A field of clover emits precious sweetness no perfume can capture.

Excitement and euphoria, the anticipation of and immediate reaction to overconsumption, are momentary. So is the thing consumed. With fewer things there is less anticipation. There is less maintenance too. Without the striving for the next thing, there is more time. Time for love, time for thought, time for gratitude. This time is the life of the spirit, and its passage is sweet.

Today I will notice the creations
of my mind and spirit.

Do not promise yourself or the world good
for future generations if you have not hope for the
present in the use of the means put into your hands.
Work for the living with all your might.

Unknown

It is not enough to know what is right (and what is wrong). It is
not enough to understand that injustice is done to our sisters and
brothers in the name of law and order. It is not enough to grumble
over the morning coffee that the world is coming to a sorry end.

We must do what we can in our little corner of it. That does not
necessarily mean moving to a different location or changing jobs or
religious communities so that we can campaign in the most obvious
arena. It does not mean changing anything material. It does mean
that we must examine our own fears and apprehensions to sweep
our inner houses clean of prejudice and injustice.

We must model kindness for our children, our parents and our
co-workers. We must conserve the resources the earth has provided so that we and other living creatures can continue to call it our
home. We must work for the living with all our might.

One way I can work for the living
is _____ .

We learned that service is the rent we pay
for living. It is the very purpose of life and not
something you do in your spare time.

Marion Wright Edelman

Spare-time service is all I can afford when I am striving for
recognition. When I get wrapped up in the importance of my own
schedule, my own commitments, my own importance, I don't have
time to do much more for others than to write a cursory note or
contribute commercially baked sweets to an occasion. There is
nothing wrong with the notes or the sweets. It is the spareness of
the time I want to change.

What I want for my life is that it be a life of service, not just
moments sprinkled here and there. I want to serve the people and
causes that have brought richness and passion into the life I live. I
don't mean goody-two-shoes self-negating service. I want more
time with the music that lifts me, the child who grows older, the
places that seem spiritual.

This may require that I spend less time striving and acquiring and
that I have less to maintain. It surely means a re-evaluation of my
priorities and more focused attention on the service of the beautiful
music, growing children and majestic environment I say I value.

*Do I spend my days in the service of those
things and people I hold dear?*

If we accept being woman, man, withdrawn or
all-managing, of this race or that, and make of it
completeness, encompassing all the nobilities
and humiliations of which we alone are capable, then
what self-respect we could develop, what cause
we could have for paying respect to one another,
to exchange courtesy and compassion.

Florida Scott-Maxwell

It seems to me that the meaning of community has changed. Where once—not so long ago—it meant family, or town, or at least geographic area, it now means special interest group, or a group based on ethnic origin. I don't think this is bad, but I do think it threatens many of us.

If my community is my sisters, as defined by politics (African-American sisters or literary sisters), then my biological or adoptive sister may not be in my primary community. By the same token, if my community is my work buddies, it may not include my spouse or my children. The problem may be that my work buddies and I don't talk with my literary sisters or with my spouse or children.

Simplifying my life includes spending time with those people with whom I am most myself. I am most comfortable among them and I do not have to explain myself. I also have a responsibility to find ways to connect communities so that the groups to which I belong do not get isolated from other communities.

*If we can talk and listen between and among
communities, we can create a larger community of
sisters and brothers, plants and animals,
animate and inanimate things.*

————————————— ❧ —————————————

What you can accumulate is never real
because when you accumulate you're not free.
Freedom is in awareness.

Tara Singh

————————————— ❧ —————————————

What I can accumulate may make me physically comfortable or feel psychologically secure, but accumulation does not expand my freedom after basic needs are met. A large home is a responsibility. Cars have to be maintained. Closets full of clothes require pressing, cleaning, choosing. Too many choices and too much obligation add up to a lot of time attending to things and not much time attending to life.

Finding the right balance between material things that make me happy and add to the pleasure and excitement I feel in life, and the time to learn, grow, change, appreciate and be, is delicate. Where I have erred on the side of things I thought would make me happy, I'd like to slide to the other side of the fulcrum and choose time to enjoy what life is, right now.

I have more than I need of things and less than
I want of time to enjoy people, solitude,
the world around me.

I just surround myself with people
who want what I want.

Dick Vermiel

For so much of our time we have little chance to choose those around us. Co-workers, neighbors, even family members are usually "givens" in our worlds. But when we do have a say—when our associations are voluntary—whom do we choose?

Do a little observation of humankind. Next time you experience someone who is deeply dissatisfied with life or someone who is confidently pursuing her or his own dream, notice with whom they associate. See if your observations confirm that unhappy people tend to associate with other unhappy people and that those who are joyously focused on their fondest dreams are surrounded by people doing the same.

This is not a suggestion to avoid those who have beliefs or goals different from ours, nor a call to surround ourselves with homogeneity—not at all. To live in a community is to benefit from differences.

This is a reminder of the powerful influence of those with whom we spend time. When we have a choice, let us choose those who will reinforce us, nurture us and encourage us on our journey.

*I will seek out those who share
my dream and vision.*

—————————————— ❧ ——————————————

Language has created the word "loneliness"
to express the pain of being alone, and the word
"solitude" to express the glory of being alone.

Paul Tillich

—————————————— ❧ ——————————————

There are some states for which both the word loneliness and the word solitude seem to apply. My father died this year and lonely is the word I would use to describe myself much of the time. I am struck now at holidays when calling Mom and Dad, or traveling to see them, that I am traveling to or calling one, not two. Even though I have always been closer to my mother, his absence makes me feel both lonely and vulnerable in ways I have not felt before.

I watch my mother carefully. It is for her that both words seem to apply. She is alone in a house they built together. And sometimes, particularly family times, she is certainly lonely. She says she cannot go to church without crying. I could not for months sing a hymn without choking on the memory of singing hymns with my dad. I see her cry and I know that memories of other times have made her sad, and lonely too. But sometimes, after having spent years attending to his physical needs, she begins to experience the glory of being alone—at least I hope so. To enjoy the absence of responsibility for others, her children, her mother, then her husband, may blossom into an enjoyment, even a glory, in being alone.

To experience the peace of solitude,
perhaps we need to walk through
the anguish of loneliness.

*Simplicity begins with a letting go—
not a letting go of the value of things, or the
pleasure of things, but rather a letting go
of the possession of things.*

Michael Hechmer

Only very recently have I been willing to consider the wisdom of Larry's caution about things and how things have a way of possessing us as well as our believing that we possess them. Since we spent a peaceful weekend at a retreat house in the country where there was no distraction from the beauty of nature or the sound of our own thoughts, I have sought to protect in my "regular" life some of the calm I felt there.

We have had a snow storm, of course, which is normal for winter in Minnesota, and the snowblower quit halfway through the driveway. Larry spent one Sunday afternoon fixing it before I heard the surge of its motor again. We had the carpet cleaned after the cat and four adults tramped on it for too long. And now I am aware of the grit from the sidewalks and the dirty snow we have tracked inside onto the clean carpet. So I am vacuuming more. It goes on and on.

I am not suggesting that I or anyone let those things we possess go to wrack and ruin. I am suggesting to myself that I consider the cost of maintaining the thing, or protecting the thing before and in addition to the pleasure and the value of the thing.

*Each material pleasure I add to my
environment must be bought at the corresponding
subtraction of my time to maintain it.*

---   ❧   ---

Look for companions who are willing to
search for themselves.

Stephen C. Paul

---   ❧   ---

At a critical time in my life one of my important companions invited my mother to take part in my change process. My mother, to her credit, replied honestly that she was sure this would be good for her but she did not have the courage to change. Even then I knew it took a fair amount of courage for her to stand firm in her own self-understanding.

For so much of my life I have been blown like a dried and weightless leaf in the winds of other people's expectations of me. It is simpler, although not as easy, to examine my own life desires and commitments, to search my own heart and mind for myself. Sometimes the resulting decision means that I disappoint my family, my friends, my colleagues.

In the effort to learn to search for myself, my mother and my husband have been good teachers. The catch for me is that both of them are important to me and I do not want to hurt or disappoint either. The tension between what my husband or mother wants and what I want for myself has sometimes been powerful. Both have almost always suggested that I follow my own path even when it leads in a different direction from theirs. To believe that and then decide when to act on their behalf or on my own has been an awesome process.

Our most important teachers model our
most important lessons.

_In the popular mind, the phrase simple living
has often been associated with self-denial. . . .
In reality the phrase can just as easily be associated
not with what is lost, but with what is gained._

Frank Levering and Wanda Urbanska

Gaining rather than giving up—I would like that. It is a helpful, positive way to approach simplifying and focusing my life. Imagine what I could acquire by sloughing off a layer from time to time as the snake does.

I could acquire freedom—freedom to do more of what I would like and less of what I imagine I have to, freedom from the expectations of others, freedom from some of the expectations I have had for myself.

I could acquire time. Though time cannot actually be acquired, it can be reallocated. I could take time from keeping up a large yard and shift it to watching birds and taking pictures. I could take time from television and newspapers and instead devote it to the reading that is important to me. I could spend less time working and more recreating.

I could acquire peace and create balance, as I move from attending to things that matter little to those that matter most, move from involvements that deplete to involvements that replenish and attend to work and family, service and recreation, friends and my own spirituality.

_By simplifying my life, I can acquire
important things._

You alone can do it, but you
cannot do it alone.

O. Hobart Mowrer

This is one of the great paradoxes of success: that I am the one responsible for making things happen in my life and you are the one responsible in your life, but neither one of us can make the things happen that we want to happen without a hand from others. We are responsible but not sufficient.

We set the course, but we cannot sail the ship by ourselves. We need assistance from parents, mates, family, friends, colleagues, professionals and occasionally even strangers.

Sometimes living out this paradox requires some relearning on our part. We may have been taught not to trust others or that it is weak to rely on them. Maybe we never learned how to involve others in productive ways; asking for help may be difficult. Our culture certainly has a clear theme of self-reliance woven into it. It is considered desirable, and better, to make it on our own. We may need to overcome these "learnings" to get to where we really want to be. Others might even help us do this.

It is okay, it is necessary and it is healthy to invite others to help you on your way.

---

*Would that life were like the shadow cast
by a wall or a tree, but it is like the
shadow cast by a bird in flight.*

The Talmud

One of the recurring themes for organizations and people these days is change. Almost all leadership and management books counsel flexibility and adaptability to change. So much change has already occurred for those who are young, and certainly for those who are older, that we hardly recognize the way things were 10 or 15 years ago.

In my professional life I try to help people deal with the responses they have to change. None of us likes to learn a new way when the old way, the shadow cast by the wall, seems just fine. Even when the old way doesn't work very well, it works in a way we understand so we don't necessarily want to go through the uncomfortable learning process of change.

To be able to change with ease, to take advantage of new opportunities, we must not be so attached to things as they are. When our lives are simpler this seems to be possible. When I am unencumbered by expectations of how things should be, or how I should be, I am freer to experiment and to flounder until I find some way that fits current needs. With fewer possessions, fewer obligations and fewer needs, I can follow the bird's shadow more easily than when I am weighed down by the stuff I have collected and thus bound to the shadow cast by the wall.

*There is freedom and lightness in change
as well as awkwardness and fear.*

Our purpose here is to wake up,
to begin to remember the powerful and
loving beings we really are. . . .

Shakti Gawain

Am I asleep, cut off from my true nature and its power? Do I
need a wake-up call? It is widely acknowledged that we use only a
fraction of our brain, our mental power. Might it also be true that
we tap into just a small portion of our emotional and spiritual
power as well?

What would it be like to experience, benefit from and use much
more of this? Exciting. Scary. Powerful. Awe-ful. Like living on a different plane. Revolutionary.

Would I give more of myself and my resources? Would I experience others in new ways? Would I have more experiences that I
consider spiritual, rooted in the divine? Could I help accomplish
things I previously considered unlikely, unthinkable?

How will I know if I am awake or need the wake-up call? Will I
be aware and listening when the call arrives? Will I answer the call?

When the call comes, I hope I am tuned
in well enough to hear it.

4

Vocation

V ocation can mean paid work, but it doesn't necessarily. It might also mean a deep volunteer commitment. The word vocation comes from a Latin word meaning to call: it is that work which gives our life meaning, to which we want to devote most energy and from which we get our deepest satisfaction, our calling.

It takes a long time for some to find their vocation. Work presents itself in many forms, and grabbing onto some form of it doesn't seem to be a problem for most. The problem may come in identifying what it is about any work that gives meaning to life and from which we get satisfaction.

It took many years for me to understand I had to uncover or discover the work which gives my life meaning, and to understand that just any work wouldn't automatically give life meaning. Prior to my finding my vocation, I worked at many things. I enjoyed each one (sometimes immensely) for a time, and then I felt used up or bored.

I didn't understand that I needed to align who I was with what I did or do.

It has taken most of my chronological adulthood to align my being and my doing, and it has been an intentional journey of self-revelation. In my experience with other adults who are confirming or uncovering their own vocation, it is the intentionality that's important. I might guess in a minute what I'm meant to do and what satisfies me. It might take hours, or years, of being in the process to understand it. The time it takes isn't important, although it can be frustrating to know one's vocation has not been uncovered. The willingness to uncover it is important.

Once having found a vocation, options broaden rather than narrow. I have found that my vocation is teaching. I have vocational training in both elementary education and ministry. Yet it took a long time to discover that teaching in a formal way was not my vocation. I have taught pre-school, student taught in a third grade, tutored at the junior high level and served as lay preacher in my church. Based on both the education and the experience, I eliminated formal contexts (the classroom, the church sanctuary) of teaching as my vocation.

Only when I could view teaching as a broad concept that included children and adults, experiential and instructional learning, indoors and outside, academic and on-the-job—well, you get the picture—could I see that teaching was my vocation.

A vocation once discovered might be a groove in which we operate comfortably—sometimes without consciousness—but it shouldn't be a rut. If we are bored and enervated by our vocation, chances are we haven't got it quite right or we have changed, grown or matured beyond a vocation that once fit. It's time to find another or to modify the one that gives meaning so that our excitement and commitment are new again.

It's not always possible to achieve this commitment in a job. My husband would most like to live his life taking pictures of lichen and bark and running water and birds in the woods. So far he hasn't found a way to make a living at this, and so he does his second favorite thing to make a living and his first favorite on vacations and in his leisure time.

Vocation can be all-consuming. In my present job, a job so closely aligned with who I am that I lose myself in it, I get used up because I put so much into it. So even though I have found a job that really is my vocation, I must be aware of balance or lack of balance with my relationships and my need for self-renewal. Either Mae West or Tullulah Bankhead said, "Too much of a good thing is wonderful," and perhaps much of the time that is true. It's also true that too much vocation is often described as workaholism, and it can destroy families and health. Discovering and living a vocation are enriching pursuits. Balancing vocation with love, leisure and laughter enrich the vocation and the person even more.

We write of vocation because that calling to which each of us is summoned can give focus and meaning to our lives. It is the ground from which we harvest our talents and skills. Finding vocation both opens our vision of possibilities and allows us to eliminate those activities that keep us busy but unsatisfied. We write of vocation to learn about ourselves and share whatever we have learned with others in the spirit of mutual discovery.

Why do you spend your money for that
which is not bread and your labor for
that which does not satisfy?

Isaiah 55:2

The old book knows us well. It foreshadowed the state we
would get ourselves into—consuming our lives in unsatisfying work
that diminishes us, and spending our substance to acquire and
maintain much more than we need.

Why do we do it?

There are many "whys." Why? Because it is part of the human
condition. Why? Because everyone else does it. Why? Because
we've been brought up to expect to. Why? Because it is necessary
to pay the bills. Why? Because we want to live the materially good
life. Why? Because work is not supposed to be satisfying. Why?
Because . . .

Despite the many whys, we are responsible for determining how
we spend our time and money—for stewardship of our resources.
From a personal viewpoint, this involves work that is satisfying and
fulfilling, that makes good use of our talents and makes us want to
get up in the morning. From a community standpoint, this entails
work that makes a contribution to our common well-being, that
helps make the world a slightly better place.

We craft such a work and lifestyle through our choices and decisions, through support and understanding from others and through
hard work. Like much in life, it is a source of great satisfaction when
our hard work pays off.

*I accept the challenge to create fulfilling
work for myself.*

Vocation . . . would include finding out the
place where the need of the world coincides with
your own gifts, where that which you can
give joyfully is received joyfully.

Sam Keen

Isn't that a wonderful vision—a world of work with an intersection where your giving and the world's receiving coincide? What a revolution of spirit would be wrought if the schools taught us to find that place and prepared us to work in it. What a true sense of calling each would have and experience in that giving and receiving. What high ground from which to begin each day.

Imagine what it takes for that to happen. First you have to know your gifts, then you have to be ready to use them in the world. Next you have to find a place where your gifts are needed, and finally the people in that place have to be happy with what you are giving.

I actually have days like that—once in awhile. And I can tell you they sure beat the other kind of days.

I will strive to have more days like that
and to put myself in places where
it happens more often.

A bad day fishing beats a
good day at work.

Bumper Sticker

You fill in the blank: A bad day _____ beats a good day at work. A bad day on the golf course, a bad day watching birds, a bad day doing needlepoint, a bad day with the grandchildren? It's a part of our culture that we are not supposed to like work. After all, why do you think they call it "work"? If it was supposed to be enjoyable, it would be called "fun"! Right?

It is ironic that we in the United States should espouse this "work is a necessary evil" attitude at a time when we are working more than we have in the last 40 years and when workaholism doesn't seem to be in decline.

When we view and pursue our work as a necessary evil—as something we do for most of the week so we can do what we want for the remainder of the week, as the first thing we would discard if we won the lottery—it becomes something that detracts from, rather than contributes, to our lives.

When we live in balance, we embrace work as a vital component of our lives, as an essential element in a life of wholeness. We create such work for ourselves so we can express who we are and what we value and so we can make a contribution to society by creating and providing something that supports our life as a community.

*A good day fishing and a good day
at work go together.*

❧
Do what you love,
the money will follow.

Marsha Sinetar
❧

In my photography class the other night a man introduced himself by saying, "I've been a successful realtor for 17 years and I want to spend the rest of my life doing something I love—taking pictures."

Imbedded in this statement is a new criterion for work—doing what you love. Many of us started out doing something we loved, but somehow along the way it changed or we changed, and now instead of life-giving it is life-draining. A few have come to believe that doing what they love is intended for after hours or is impossible.

But many seem to be leaving their "real" jobs to take pictures, lead rafting trips, raise goats in Montana, start their own businesses. Finding and pursuing work that flows from us, is us, is important because in our culture our work says so much about who we are and takes up so much of our day.

Notice that Sinetar says the money will follow—not gush, not flood, not inundate—but follow, result from, come later. In fact she says the lag time is sometimes very long. I have been working independently for six years and, although I keep getting closer, I have yet to make as much money as I did when I worked for someone else.

No matter what you call it—your bliss, passion, mission or ministry—the key is that you do it because you love it, not because it gives you the most prestige, or makes your father proud, or lets you build up a healthy retirement fund. This is not a formula for success in the world's terms, but it is a formula for joy, satisfaction and contribution.

I acknowledge that doing what
I love is possible.

———————— ❦ ————————

This is the time of harvest, of
thanksgiving and joy, of leave-taking and sorrow.
Now day and night are equal, in perfect balance,
and we give thought to the balance and
flow within our own lives.

Starhawk

———————— ❦ ————————

We harvest the fruits of our work as well as the fruits of our gardens. There is a time for achievement and a time for tending our crops. Driving along freeways, it is easier to see the growth of farmers' corn or wheat, easier to measure the progress of the tractor as it moves between the rows, than it is to see our own growth and ripening.

Achievements, awards, winning are all signs that we have grown in some way, that we have ripened. But inevitably, beyond the harvest, is a time for rest and renewal. Restlessness in a relationship, boredom on a job, frustration with an obligation may all be signs of a need to rest and renew.

Sometimes we cannot repeat the feats that brought us joy or success in the past. Sometimes we don't want to. Giving ourselves enough time—giving ourselves winter—to renew and to begin again is a human need as well as nature's.

The earth must rest as we must.
Creativity comes out of what appears to be barrenness.
Frozen ground produces fragrant blossoms.
Balance means celebrating the inertia
as well as the buds.

When the artist is truly the servant of the work,
the work is better than the artist.

Madeleine L'Engle

Being a servant of a kind of work, in the positive sense of service, means having both commitment and concentration. It doesn't
matter what the work is. It is possible to be an artist in a toll booth,
on a construction site or in a classroom.

The artist has an attitude of reverence for the tasks defined by
work and a spirit of gift-giving toward those who come in contact
with the work. This may mean that the toll taker lends a nickel, or
the construction worker fits steel joints together with the care of a
surgeon, or the teacher creates different environments for learning
so students with different preferences will learn.

The work, then, is better than the artist who serves it because the
work contains the personality of the artist. That personality is
infused by being relinquished to the work. It is only possible to do
this by noticing in which activities one loses oneself and to entrust
one's ego to the pursuit of those activities.

*I will notice my attitude toward
my present work and toward the activities
to which I give myself.*

There is something in every one of you
that waits and listens for the sound
of the genuine in yourself.

Howard Thurman

How can we wait and listen for the genuine in ourselves? When I am sitting at my computer, my fingers flying across the keys because I cannot get my thoughts on the screen fast enough, I lose all sense of time. Perhaps this is an expression of the genuine in myself. When I sob out loud in movies because I am so involved in the injustice of the life on the screen even though I know it is just a story, I am expressing something deep and genuine in myself.

All of us have these expressions. Mihaly Csikszentmihalyi called them "flow" in a book of the same title. The Bible may be describing them when Jesus says that we must lose ourselves before we can be found. Traditional Christianity has equated losing ourselves with a life of selfless service. Perhaps another meaning is losing ourselves to our most genuine self.

Paying attention to when this happens and how to lose ourselves in this sense more of the time, rather than less, is a challenge. Popular books promise us we will find material security if we "follow our bliss." There is some evidence of this in our culture, but the more overwhelming evidence is that we will find spiritual wholeness.

*If learning to find the genuine in myself does
not add one cent to my paycheck, it adds
uncountable riches to my spirit.*

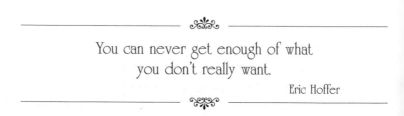

You can never get enough of what
you don't really want.

Eric Hoffer

A close friend reminds me that if my mouth is watering for pistachio ice cream, eating a gallon of chocolate chip just won't satisfy my craving. It probably won't satisfy my waistband either, but that's not really the point. The friend reminds me of this "Hofferism" when I am tempted to give up on something I really want for the future in favor of something I can achieve in the present.

I no longer wish to work in the kinds of places that once made me want to get up in the morning. My taste for work has not diminished but my taste for politics and rules has. It is therefore an opportune, if frightening, time for me to create the work life I have been saying I wanted for several years. I want pistachio work, but I am often tempted to settle for chocolate chip.

There are all kinds of reasons. Money underlies most of them. Yet part of the reason I do not want to work in environments where I once worked is that I want to pare down spiritually and materially. I want to get to the core of my talents and needs, spend time with people I really care about, and spend time doing and thinking about things I think are important. A little voice says, "Nobody gets to do that, what makes you think you can?" This is just one more reason not to wait for and work toward pistachio.

I am grateful for the opportunity to
focus on my talents.

Most of us go to our graves with
our music still inside us.

Oliver Wendell Holmes

Whan song are you singing when you feel fully alive, in tune with life and making your best contribution? Are you singing that song regularly—right now—or is it inside of you chafing to be let out?

When is it that you are really being you—taking striking pictures, giving empowering speeches, founding a business, organizing an Elderhostel program, building for Habitat for Humanity, feeding hungry people, going to seminary, being a nurturing parent or supportive friend, being really good at your work? People's music is as various as people themselves.

Some of us were blessed with families and surroundings that encouraged us to broadcast our tune and lyrics. Others were discouraged from doing so because it was unrealistic, even foolish. Unsure of our own music, some of us adopted whatever was on the hit parade as our own.

The marvel of today is that we can sing our song and play our music anytime, even if right now we only have a few moments. What a wonderful possibility!

*I will listen to my music more closely and
find a way to express it today.*

Work is one of our greatest opportunities
to contribute to the well-being of ourselves
and our community. . . .

                                        Tom Bender

Satisfying work that makes a contribution is a key to harmonious living. What a difference it makes in our lives. Creating and sustaining this for ourselves is a major task of adult life. In our culture, it may require that we swim upstream because the message we often get is that work is supposed to be a drag and a burden.

In my consulting work I find increasing numbers of people in all areas of organizations saying things such as, "I dread coming to work in the morning" or, "Work isn't fun anymore." They don't believe that work is supposed to be like a party or a comedy film, but they have experienced a loss of positive challenge and feel they no longer make a difference. They are not fulfilled and full of energy; they are discouraged, burned-out, depleted and stuck.

What a powerful coming together it is when our work contributes both to us and our community. We have a sense of satisfaction, fulfillment and excitement about it. And we are making a difference—our little corner of the world is a better place because of what we are doing.

*I will create and re-create work that is
fulfilling for me and makes a
contribution to others.*

---
*If you lose yourself in your work,
you find who you are.*

Frederick Buechner

There are two ways to lose yourself in your work, or anywhere else for that matter. One is to have work take up so much of you— so much of your time, energy and spirit—that it is drudgery and there is not much left for what you believe in and value. Here you find yourself by default, by definitely knowing that your work hides who you are. This way of finding yourself feels lousy.

The other way is for your work to be an expression of who you are. Then you plow into work and stay at it long hours, not because you are overwhelmed or fearful, but because you enjoy it. Then work is energizing and absorbing. You may even lose track of time and place for awhile. This way of finding yourself feels good.

Either way you learn something about you and about the importance of fulfilling work.

*May you find yourself by losing yourself
in joyous concentration.*

—————————————— ❧ ——————————————

The environment that the organization
worries about is put there by
the organization.

Karl Weik

—————————————— ❧ ——————————————

Part of my work is to listen to other people speak about what
conditions of their work they would like to change. Often I listen
to assess a department's ability to change, which means its people's
ability or willingness to change. I don't know as well as the department how employees got into a certain way of doing things. But it
is usually fairly obvious how they could get out of it.

Sometimes the obvious is that management should change.
Often the obvious is for everyone to adapt to change and get on
with what present reality dictates. How easy it is for me to see the
organization's continuing resistance to an environment they themselves created at some point in the past. How hard it is for me to
see the prisons I have built around myself so that I will not or do
not have to change.

For most of my adult life I have been jealous of the attention my
father paid my brother. Oh what a prison I built around myself as
an explanation of Dad's preference! My family environment had
such power to hurt me because I defined it in the way I did. Only
with Dad's death was I willing to change the environment I had
made.

Even though we do not remember,
the environment we do not like is often
the environment we made.

There are at least two ways to deal with
people when things go wrong. Analyzing and
establishing blame is one; getting at the root of
the conflicting perceptions and feelings, expressing
them, and then responding is another.

Carol Frenier

I have spent much of the day wondering why my customers
want to create their own programs rather than using the services I
am prepared to provide for them. Can't they see they are reinvent-
ing the wheel, over and over again? It seems that some of them see
me as a competitor rather than a partner.

It was only at the end of the day, when I was talking with another department head about some material she had shared with me,
that I had an inspiration. I had been thinking about her as a competitor in just the same way I assume my customers have been
thinking about me.

Then I thought: I have a choice about how I respond to my colleagues and customers. If I ask for their insights and their assistance,
as I chose to do in my conversation with the department head, perhaps I could contribute to a different environment. Perhaps I have
in some way contributed to the environment of competition that
now exists.

Communication is not difficult.
It is we who make it so.

There's no off-season anymore.

Nolan Ryan

When I first began to work in financial services, I seemed to work all the time. I was looking for clients when I was not actually at work and I was working with clients when I was at work. Even when I went on vacation, I was aware that I was supposed to be "prospecting."

My first holiday season was a different story. I came in at the regular time the day after Christmas to find I was the first, and only, employee in the office. A few straggled in as the hours wore on, but we never reached full complement all week. Folks who were usually dressed in starched shirts came in sweatshirts and boating shoes. It was off-season.

In my current position, still in financial services, there was a similar looseness to the post-holiday week. But ever since it has felt like we all have worked at double time to make up for that short breather. If the 80s were a time of overwork to achieve enormous personal wealth, then the 90s seem to be a time of overwork just to keep our jobs.

Tonight I spoke with my mother and each of my three daughters on the phone and I felt guilty that those conversations kept me from my work (now possible with a laptop computer), the work I did not get done in the nine hours I spent at my desk during the day.

This is not my idea of living simply!

*Working isn't everything and certainly isn't
the only thing I want in my life.*

Dedication to love of work is evoked by
quality and is the force that energizes
high-performing systems.

Warren Bennis

It is Saturday afternoon and I sit in my living room on one of the first beautiful days of the year, writing on my laptop computer. As the pointer pulses at me I decide, moment by moment, what I want to say. This is my work. It has always been part of my work. It is a way for my extroverted self to communicate with the rest of my personality, and with a larger number of other humans than I could speak to in a lifetime.

When I am immersed in the writing, the beauty of the day only adds to the pleasure of my work. My cat purrs happily at my elbow. My mind speaks out loud to the computer screen. I am in flow, the working state of ecstasy. And the words are good. For others the words might be hammer and nails, paint and brushes or eggs and a copper bowl.

We work a lot in our house. Our "system" is high-performing at least some of the time. And at least some of the work my husband and I do in our house is work for which we are not paid. It is the work we are devoted to and from which we derive great satisfaction.

I will enjoy the flow of my
work when it is there.

Disorder can play a critical role in giving
birth to new, higher forms of order.

Margaret J. Wheatley

Transition is so messy. For six months a new job has engulfed me. Piles of source material, courses I need to learn, information I have had no time to read, much less attend to, have littered my desk. My side of the bed looks as if a book store exploded and left its debris scattered over my floor and bedside table. More piles of books and magazines that once fit neatly under the table have crept out along my clothes closet's edge.

My brain feels too full most of the time and I am afraid I will forget the important things in it. I am also afraid I will not remember which are the important things. Endless notes and reminders fill my daily calendar. I am exhausted most of the time.

I love what I do, both the job for which I am paid and the work and play I do for my own pleasure and the pursuit of a future career. But I am stretched very close to the farthest limits of my energy. I want to be able to see down the road to a day when there is more order and more balance because the disorder of this transition is over.

Patience with myself through the messy
transition to new work will relieve
some of my anxiety.

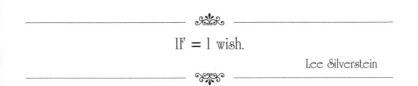

IF = I wish.

Lee Silverstein

If I did not have to work this weekend, perhaps I could rest up and have some fun so that when Monday comes I will be ready with enthusiasm to work again. Hmmm. I wish I did not have to work this weekend. Who is in control here? Right now it appears that my job is.

When we decided as a couple that we would intentionally simplify our lives, I had a job that interested me but did not spill over into nights and weekends. Now my job is fascinating and consuming. I long for the days, not so long ago, when I left the office at five and never gave work a thought on weekends. If only I could have both a job I loved and relaxation/alone time.

No one at work has put this pressure on me. My supervisor has recently suggested I cut back on a project she had given me. So why am I so consumed with working all the time?

There are lots of reasons. Some of them, I suspect, are good ones. But IF I want to simplify my life, working twelve hours a day, six days a week is not what I wish. And IF I am serious about simplicity, then "I wish" must change to "I will."

*I will look for ways to delegate and
reduce work so that my life
is more balanced.*

Companies must find new ways to harness soul-searching on the job, not just gloss over or merely avoid it.

Martha Nichols

So much of what is being written about organizations and management these days tells the reader that it is time for employers to pay attention to the whole person instead of just the person's skills. At the same time, business periodicals tell us that workers should think of themselves as business owners—with themselves as the product—because there isn't any job security anymore. Which is true: that corporations must care more about their people or that their people need to care more about themselves due to a continuing trend of reduction in the permanent workforce?

These questions relate to voluntary simplicity in this way: If I am my own business, just what is the business and to whom do I market it/me? My business is a set of communication skills I take anywhere. I don't need a corner office downtown to confirm these abilities. A straight-backed chair in the sun and a writing surface will do.

If businesses are going to encourage us to be whole people at work, there is a heap of communication that companies did not have to hear in the past that they will hear now. My business is to help teams and companies communicate so that interaction is healthy and productive. My business is also to work toward a lifestyle that keeps me healthy and productive, a lifestyle spent more in nature and less in skyscrapers.

I can feel the breeze off the lake already.

Everyone lives by selling something.

Robert Louis Stevenson

This so struck me when I read it. I have been a salesperson by profession for most of my adult life and I feel strongly that it is an honorable and honest way to live and make a living. We all sell. Pastors do, as do hairdressers, professors and coaches. Directors sell and writers languish if they don't. But selling so often has a bad name.

Selling is simple. First, the best salespeople love their product: the pastor or rabbi loves God; the director loves film or theater and acting; the professor loves his or her special area of study; and the writer loves words. Second, the salesperson loves to share the product with others. If it can help you be better at whatever you do or get whatever you want, then we both benefit. If it isn't right for you, perhaps it will benefit someone you know.

When people who call themselves salespeople try to maneuver me into a purchase or a change I don't want, don't need or can't afford, I won't buy and I won't recommend that person or the company to others I know. If I am respected and informed, I will tell others, whether I buy or not. It really is so simple.

Selling is often the most direct
way to connect people.

Harmony

5

❦

Harmony

I 'm in a city park watching birds. Other people are sitting on benches, strolling slowly around a small pond or relaxing under trees, trying to get a little relief from the sun and intense heat. Three boys appear; by looks and age they seem to be brothers. Though the park is quite well-kept and clean, they are able to find a few sticks and stones that they proceed to throw at the turtles in the pond.

In and of itself, this scene is not remarkable. It is not unusual for children (and sadly even some adults) to pester and try to harm animals. As a grade schooler I used to shoot birds with my B-B gun, though as an avid birder I now am quite embarrassed to say that I did.

What made this particular incident more remarkable was that it did not take place in the U.S., but rather in a park halfway around the world from my home in Minnesota. I was struck by the commonality of young boys' behavior toward vulnerable animals. I wondered why young Asian boys as well as young North American boys throw sticks at turtles and shoot at birds.

It also made me begin to think about harmony and the interconnectedness of all life. What a compelling idea; how difficult to live it out. Living in peace with other people—the people in our daily lives, in our homes and workplaces, and people around the world whom we don't even know—is one of the major facets of harmony. It is an ideal that is imbedded in many religious and philosophical traditions. And it is a constant challenge to live out. Accepting and not judging the differences among us is a first step.

Acceptance allows us to appreciate that these differences form the strands of the human tapestry. One need only glance at a newspaper to notice that we don't yet do this very well in our world, our communities, our neighborhoods or our families.

Harmony also entails living in ways that respect nonhuman life—mammals, birds, reptiles, plants and even insects. It acknowledges our unity and interconnectedness with all living things and asks us to accept all creatures as part of the mystery of life. When we celebrate life, we celebrate all life.

I have to admit that there are some parts of life—mosquitoes come to mind quite readily—that are a conundrum to me. What do they add to the whole, what do they bring to the party? Perhaps their function is to keep humans humble, I'm not sure. Must I include them in my celebrations of life?

Respect for the planet earth itself—including the air and soil and water and rocks too—is another element of harmony. Earth, after all, is our home. It alone provides what sustains our lives. We often forget that if it won't support other life—frogs and birds and fish, for example—ultimately it probably won't support human life either. I am confused, saddened, sometimes angry when others treat this planet as though there is some other planet we can all move to when this one no longer sustains us. Stewardship of earth is our calling.

At its root, harmony entails being at peace internally and having a sense of well-being (being well-connected with oneself, if you will). Being at peace with oneself is a prerequisite for being at peace with others. When we are experiencing disharmony with something outside ourselves, we may well be holding up a mirror to examine ourselves. When I holler at my cat Solomon, he is rarely the real source of my anger.

My wife and I are blessed with much harmony in our lives. We get along well with each other and, for the most part, our various families. We are part of several supportive and affirming communities that deliberately try to widen the spheres of accord that surround them. As urban neighborhoods go, ours is fairly tranquil. Increasingly we experience ourselves as an integral part of the amazing natural world.

We write of harmony because it is foundational. When it is missing, particularly internal harmony, it is very difficult to think of simplicity and balance and to make life-enhancing choices. We write of harmony because it is our hope and prayer for every human, our hope and prayer for you. We want a harmonious environment where creatures can thrive and earth itself regenerates for our grandchildren and their grandchildren, and their grandchildren too.

We write of harmony because, as a steady diet, it is better than disharmony. There is a song that goes, "Let there be peace on earth and let it begin with me." That is the only way peace and harmony can begin and be sustained, with each of us acknowledging and acting upon the holy yet fragile inter-connectedness of all life.

All things are connected. Whatever befalls the
earth befalls the [people] of earth.

attributed to Chief Seattle

The societal lifestyle we have crafted minimizes our interconnectedness with all life. In the United States we use resources as
though there is no tomorrow and no other people who will need
them.

Often we are blind to our place in the web of life. So we don't
recognize that lakes that are not healthy for fish are probably not
healthy for us, and that if there is no place to support life for a
whooping crane or a wolf, one day there may not be a place that
will support life for our great-grandchildren.

We presume that it can't happen—won't happen—to us, that
there will always be drinkable water when we turn on the tap,
cheap gasoline when we go to the pump and breathable air when
we open the window. By any measure, we consume more than our
fair share of what the earth provides.

Committing to live simply will help to right the balance. We will
consciously use less and make choices that help ensure that this
planet will be vital for coming generations.

I can be mindful of my "automatic" ways of
consuming and take steps to become a better steward
of what I have been provided.

It would seem ridiculous to most people to
imagine that a beach could be claimed through
ancestral right by a beach flea or a bird, and
that it would be barren without them.

John Hay

As a bird watcher, I certainly can appreciate that the beach would be barren without birds. When I am "birding," they are the center of my focus, the center of my universe for that time, and the slightest movement catches my attention. When I have set aside some time for birding and am unable to locate many, I am disappointed.

But beach fleas (actually small crustaceans), I can do without. And annoying insects such as black flies or gnats, I wouldn't miss them. When they are missing I enjoy the beach more.

I don't stop to think that the birds need something to eat—something such as beach fleas or insects or fish. I forget that an absence of insects does not necessarily bode well for birds and hence for me. Insects or other things to eat are one of the conditions of satisfaction for birds, just as having interesting birds to observe is one for me.

We are part of the world of nature. Nature forms a web of interconnected parts; change and movement anywhere on the web affect each strand. If I want birds, I need to understand deeply and defend the prerogative of the beach flea.

Today I will examine the web of life for an unlikely
way my life is connected to other life.

I have often noticed that these things, which
obsess me, neither bother nor impress other people
even slightly. I am horribly apt to approach some
innocent at a gathering . . . and say, "Do you know
that in the head of the caterpillar of the ordinary
goat moth there are two hundred twenty-eight
separate muscles?" The poor wretch flees. I am not
making chatter; I mean to change his life.

Annie Dillard

Imagine that—228 muscles in the head of a caterpillar. Can you picture where all those muscles would be and what they would do? I'm not sure I can.

To me it is incredible that a caterpillar has that many muscles— and equally incredible that someone knows that it has them. Most of us probably wouldn't even notice a caterpillar unless we found it on a plant in the garden.

Could that fact—or one of the thousands like it (the migration of terns from pole to pole, the number of galaxies in the universe)— actually touch your life, be of significance to you? Could knowing and appreciating that raise your sense of affiliation with other living things? Might it heighten your awareness of the need for all creatures to have a place that sustains them? Could it intensify your sense of awe? Would it make you think twice before squishing a caterpillar?

Today I will look for a hidden
miracle in my world.

――――――――――――――― ⚜ ―――――――――――――――

Whatever comes to pass in our human world,
there is no shadow of us cast upon the rising sun,
no pause in the flowing of the winds or halt in the
long rhythms of the breakers hastening ashore.

                                        Henry Beston

――――――――――――――― ⚜ ―――――――――――――――

I am often restored, renewed and healed in nature. Several of
my most clearly spiritual moments have been outdoors.

One fall, during a weekend retreat, I sat on a stump immersed
up to my waist in a sleeping bag watching leaves fall from the trees.
The paths they took during descent intrigued me. Some spiraled
like cork screws, others fluttered back and forth within an invisible
vertical corridor, still others went quickly and directly away from the
trunk as if desiring to get as far away from their birth place as possible. Patterns in the woods, cycles of life and death and preparation for rebirth occur without authority of humans.

While looking for birds in March, I lay on my belly behind tufts
of tall grass to get out of the wind for a few minutes. The sun, once
the wind was blocked, was quite warm. I heard a noise—perhaps
a mouse?—and turned quickly to see it. Nothing. Another noise,
another quick turn . . . nothing again.

After a few rounds of this I realized that small pieces of ice were
dislodging and falling from the underside of wind-swept grass tufts.
By the time I heard the noise, the event had already happened and
my turning to see was too late. I had to be satisfied—and I was—
with the process. I was at peace and aware that we remain oblivi-
ous to much that goes on in our world.

Where I live, nature is very accessible and usually free. I want
to be in natural settings more often to reclaim my peace and balance and to be reminded of my place in the tapestry of life.

I can restore myself through simple, readily available activities.

We are here to bring to consciousness the
beauty and power that are around us and to
praise the people who are here with us.

Annie Dillard

As I raked the dry leaves from my garden, where chrysanthe-mums still abound in yellow and gold and lavender, I was aware of the beauty of the leaves and of the day. It is my joy to plant care-fully in the spring. As a lover of color who lives with a yard most-ly shaded year-round, my challenge is to choose plants that will break out in riots of purple and orange, ruby and peach without full benefit of the sun. In five years I have achieved a pretty full palette.

Each year there are surprises. I forget that I planted a little gem that emerges in late August. A squirrel will move the lily tubers some distance from where I planted them. The yarrow doesn't do well and the calendula does. Even though my expertise grows with each gardening season, much of the rebirth is out of my hands. I can tend to the weeds, place the annuals according to height and hue, and separate crowded perennials. But I cannot predict the effect of any of these things on my beautiful garden.

In learning to do these things I have sought and depended on the advice of two expert gardeners nearby. Their garden seems much more controlled than mine because they know much more and spend much more time at gardening than I do. I must say, though, that I like the surprises mine offers.

The beauty all around us is there. It is
up to us to notice and to share it.

---

*Simplicity in all things is the secret of the wilderness
and one of its most valuable lessons.*

Sigurd Olson

Even a confirmed city dweller like myself can appreciate the lessons of the wilderness. There are no phones and no air conditioning, other than the breeze that ruffles the edge of my sleeping bag or the rain that washes away the sweat of an afternoon's canoeing.

I am not a lover of large doses of the wild. I like hot showers and clean sheets. I like firm beds and no rocks under my shoulders. I invariably wrench an aging back carrying packs, even cameras, along the sun-sprinkled paths of our closest natural preserve.

But I can also hear the sound of my own soul here as I cannot in the city. My inner conversations slow down, even cease altogether. I eat whatever I have brought and not in the order of breakfast, lunch, dinner. In some ways there are fewer rules here—no rules about music after 10 p.m., no outlines due by Monday. In some ways, of course, there are more. We must hoist the food packs way up in the trees to discourage the bears. We must use or bring out everything we have brought in. We must pay careful attention to fires, wood chopping, even whittling so as not to seriously endanger ourselves or the environment. There is no fire station or emergency room within walking distance.

The quiet of these days, the smell of wildflowers, the simplicity of this time all combine to rejuvenate me for the city pace to which I return.

*I can envision the wilderness that renews
me even when I cannot get there.*

Action should culminate in wisdom.

Bhagavad Gita

Recently my well-educated stepson told me it was too late to save the rainforests of the world, that no matter what we do now, the resulting environment, albeit reforested, will be vastly different from the environment we have already fatally affected. We cannot promise the beetles and snakes that what they have eaten will return or that they will survive long enough for their food to replenish itself if it does. We cannot protect indigenous people from encroaching civilization.

It is at least sad to me that we, all people of the earth, have changed its face so dramatically in the name of progress, or necessity. Farmers in Costa Rica level the trees on steep hillsides to grow enough food or graze enough animals to sustain their families. They are not wantonly destroying natural resources to build roads or resorts. Theirs is a small world of simple needs. They are real needs. And their destruction of the forest is not a simple problem with simple solutions.

Yet our action, whatever action we take in pursuit of preserving or remaking the forest, will result in something, something evidently different from what the remaining forests are now. How can we assure the beetles and the people that our action will culminate in wisdom?

*Action without forethought and evaluation will
not often yield wisdom. Even the most
carefully planned action is not
entirely controllable.*

Love the animals, love the plants, love everything.
If you love everything, you will perceive the
divine mystery in things. Once you perceive it,
you will begin to comprehend it better every day.
And you will come at last to love the whole
world with an all-embracing love.

Fyodor Dostoyevsky

On a recent trip to Alaska the power of nature's beauty was intoxicating. The tour only included the southern peninsula, and only accommodated one day's stop in each of three small towns (small by many standards, though one was the capital city). Yet the abundance of flowers, the smell of wet soil, the gurgle of running salmon in a cold clear stream and the silence—then thunderous cracking—of brilliant blue glaciers provided long-lasting visions.

From banana slugs to bald eagles, from whales to flocks of puffins, everything seemed larger than any comparable bird, worm or mammal in any other part of the country. It was easy to love the lushness, the exotic, the new. It was easy to embrace all of life when none of it threatened.

But embracing all of life includes the great hurricanes of autumn, the separation from dear friends and the death of a child. The groaning baskets of flowers hung from street lamps in Ketchikan can in no way balance the slow death of a parent. But the love of all life can bring joy and peace even in the midst of sad anticipation.

Loving all of life is free
and attainable.

Celebrate seasonal changes, solstices and
equinoxes with special observances.

133 Ways to Save the Earth

When we notice the changes in nature, the cooler evenings of fall, the sprouting crocuses of early spring, longer days in summer, and the biting cold of winters in the north, we notice that they reappear in cycles every year.

When we anticipate seasonal changes, perhaps we can equate those changes with our own psychological and physical changes. Although we cannot physically recycle (there is no known fountain of youth), we seem to return to some core psychological issues the way seasons return to new growth or rain. We renew our energy by resting, just as the earth rests through winter in many parts of the world.

When we celebrate natural change, the celebration marks important rhythms that occur inside as well as around us. Celebrating seasonal change is a simple way to acknowledge the transitions and cycles of life.

*Today I will celebrate some aspect of growth in
the natural world as well as in me.*

--------------------- ⚜ ---------------------

A person who undertakes to grow a garden . . .
will no longer look upon rain as an impediment
of traffic, or upon the sun as a
holiday decoration.

Wendell Berry

--------------------- ⚜ ---------------------

Gardening and other outdoor activities help keep us close to the earth and remind us that we are a part of—not apart from—all life. When we are outside long enough to experience what is there—not just to rush through it to get to our garage, car, office or train—we know once again that bugs and wind and leaves and rain are all as much a part of life as we are.

Modern life, particularly urban life, makes it easy for us to forget this. Our buildings and cars buffer us from the natural world and the daily changes in it. Heaters and air conditioners protect us from temperature changes, lights make it possible to carry on our activities at any time, insecticides remove annoying bugs. We can easily deny our interdependence with the natural world.

Sunsets, migrating birds, fresh snow and moving water remind me of my place on and interdependence with the earth. But when I don't take time to experience these reminders, there are mosquitoes, bitter cold and tornadoes to jar my memory.

I will welcome rain as a necessity of life
and wind as a reminder that life is
movement and change.

It is a mystery to me why some people see
beauty and magic everywhere they look,
while others remain unmoved.

Andrew Matthews

The signals for all the radio and television shows in your locale are passing through the place you are right now, but you have to have a radio or television turned on to receive the programs.

The same is true of the beauty and magic around us. It is there all the time, but we won't notice unless we are tuned in to its presence.

What beauty and magic surround you? How about

- friends
- spring flowers
- people remaining optimistic and determined in the face of adversity
- the laughter and freedom of children
- love
- the possibility of change
- pets

just to get the list started.

To experience the enchantment, take the time to see the everyday in a special way.

The beauty and magic I will look for in my life today include _____.

---

*Summer ends, and Autumn comes, and he who
would have it otherwise would have high tide
always and a full moon every night.*

Hal Borland

Change brings new challenges as well as new delights. I think of the warm summer evenings of my youth, many of which were spent at water's edge. Some evenings when the tide was out, moon and stars shone on silvery mud beyond the sand of the beach. The smell of seaweed and sea creatures was strong and pungent. Walking out from the shore for a swim meant following the sand to the mud, feeling the muck between our toes and smelling the strong low tide smells.

Sometimes the air was heavy enough to make that trip worth it. We would have preferred perpetual high tide, of course. Later we built a pool and the problem of tides was a thing of the past. The bottom our feet touched was clean cement any time of day or night. Yet I don't miss the pool of my youth. I miss the shore.

If both our environment and our relationships stayed the same (and that state were one we could define), how would we know the deep joy of a loved one returning after an absence (of geography or emotion)? How could we experience the sweet smell of the air after a storm? As painful as life sometimes is, and I believe there is pain for all of us, there is also joy. There is a crocus in the snow, a hand squeezed in reassurance and the tide returning water to a sandy shore to show that the joy in life is worth every moment of its sorrow.

*I will look for signs of change in my environment
and in my relationships.*

Toward the end of March when the ground is
still covered with ice and snow . . . one goes into a
sort of trance. . . . Then comes a day when the sun
bursts out of the overcast and everyone stands,
even for a brief moment, to bask in its warmth. It is
miraculous . . . and as though to prove it, the
chickadees . . . sing their plaintive mating song.

Sigurd Olson

Winter has seemed especially long, cold and burdensome this year. In all parts of the country folks are saying, "We've had it!" And today—just as Olson described it—the sun has burst through to bring welcome relief. The temperature is in the mid-40s and the snow is melting.

There are other signs as well. Not only have the chickadees here begun that new song, but the cardinals have added their spring call as well. The crows, present and active all winter, were much more vocal when I went out early this morning. There are stirrings afoot.

Yet I can't let myself be fooled into thinking spring has actually arrived. Even though these signs are hopeful, it is March and in Minnesota spring doesn't really come until April or May. We can still expect snow and cold.

So let us enjoy today while we can. Perhaps more than any other thing weather can remind us to enjoy the day we have at hand, for tomorrow is literally another day and who knows what it might bring.

When I have waited for a long time, I will bask
in the moment when it finally arrives.

❦

Small things, the routine of life, take on slower
and deeper rhythms, so that one no longer feels
one is wasting time, any more than trees waste time.
In slack periods we are now busy being.
Life begins to live us, instead of us living life.
Damaris Parker-Rhodes

Can I be busy *being* instead of *doing*? Not "busy" in the sense of having my days chock full of activities or being frenetic, but in the sense of being occupied by, giving significant attention to. It is an intriguing idea, but I'm not sure I know what that means—life living me instead of me living life.

I am able to do nothing, to have idle periods, but that seems more like the absence of "doing" than it does "being." Being certainly is not something anyone ever taught me.

I guess it means accepting that we are a part of life and that, in some sense, it is bigger, more powerful than we are. That's different from the "I'm in control/I make life happen" belief that drives me many days.

As for trees wasting time—whoa—I have no idea about that. I have enough trouble with my own time management to worry about the trees.

Instead of me directing life, I am open to
feeling life flowing through me.

Seeing again my old friends here I realize
that the time has passed very quickly, and I wonder
whether we really utilize time properly. . . . every
minute is precious. This means—if you can—serve
other sentient beings. If not, at least restrain from
harming others. And in this way your daily life
becomes more peaceful and happy.

The Dalai Lama

Respect and serve other beings—at least don't harm them—and this will make life more peaceful and happy. I guess it would. If we didn't harm other beings and they didn't harm us, then we all could have a good day. Sounds simple enough. Sounds like it would work.

Sounds simple, but I imagine it isn't. It is after all a call for each of our actions, each of our words, each of our thoughts to be life affirming, life supporting, life enhancing. It calls for the elimination of getting even, blaming, superiority, meanness and prejudice. It entails not judging others' experiences by our own.

To do this I would have to view others as equally valuable to me. I would have to see myself as one part of creation and respect the needs and being of the other parts. I would have to accept John Hay's challenge to acknowledge the beach fleas' right to the beach.

Maybe it doesn't have to be quite so daunting. Today as I encounter people I can be polite and respectful. I can ask if I can be of assistance. I can listen and practice patience. I can be gentle with other creatures and with creation itself, and recognize their right to exist. I can avoid harm. There are a lot worse ways to use my time.

May I be an instrument of peace.

*True mystery is the hooded merganser on
the pond behind our house, and what
it took for her to get there.*

Sue Halpern

As an object of natural interest, birds are particularly intriguing to me. That they come in the spring and leave in the fall is amazing in itself, let alone that they reappear at the same location and, among some species, return with the same mate.

A researcher in Minnesota once told me that he tracked the fall migration of a pair of sandhill cranes. When they left Minnesota they flew to Wisconsin and joined a larger group of cranes. They then flew right over O'Hare International Airport on their way to southern Illinois. Here the couple apparently split up, with one bird going to the east coast of Florida for the winter and the other going to the west coast. In the spring, they returned to the Illinois site, amazingly found one another among the thousands of cranes there and flew back to Minnesota together. I was amazed at this tale.

Mysteries like this, involving people as well as critters, are evident around us all day. When we take a moment to stop to smell the mysteries, we can be excited, uplifted and nurtured by them.

*I will enjoy the next
mystery I see.*

Just as the life-giving rains restore
the earth after the drought, so your power will
restore the Way and give it new life. We ask
this not only for the red people but for all the
people that they might live. In ignorance and
carelessness they have walked upon Ina Maka, our
Mother. They did not understand that they are
part of all beings, the four legged, the winged,
grandfather rock, the tree people, and our
star brothers. Now the earth and all our
relations are crying out. They cry for
the help of all people.

Native American prayer

Earth and all its life and the air surrounding it do need our help.
We need

   to tread more lightly,
   to treat all creatures with kindness,
   to use no more than our fair portion of the earth's resources,
   to clean up the waters,
   to ensure fresh air,
   to share with others so their needs are met,
   to reduce our waste,
   to respect all life.

*I am entitled to no more of the earth's
bounty than any other person.*

You know waterfalls
seem so friendly,
I guess it's because
they are full of life. . . .

Terry Rowe

Though the large waterfalls I have seen—Murchsion, Niagara, Tisisat on the Blue Nile and the Grand Canyon of the Yellowstone—awe me, it is the small ones that capture me. I stood in the stream in Spearfish Canyon, South Dakota, so long one morning that my feet were numb, photographing this relatively small falls from every conceivable angle (including behind the falls itself).

I have mentally immersed myself in "falls" no more than six or eight inches high. Captured by the changing patterns of the water and how the rock looks beneath it, I photographed one at slow speeds so that the water looks like strands of fishing line.

For some perhaps primordial reason, we are often drawn to water. And I am especially drawn to falls. They seem alive and are ever changing. Falling water models life, appearing to stay the same but actually changing every second.

If only in my mind, I can enjoy a
waterfall when I want to.

Not one time, in all I've done, have I ever
asked mercy for being a girl. I've meant to be
strong. Strength just comes in one brand—you stand
up at sunrise and meet what they send you
and keep your hair combed.

Reynolds Price

I have never wished to be a boy or to have grown into a man. I enjoy being a strong woman and have always enjoyed it. That does not mean I haven't wished for the privileges men have enjoyed for no other obvious reason than that they are men.

I have lived in a transition time between roles clearly defined for women and men and roles much more elastic. Both genders have had to give up some privilege to move out of those restricted roles. In some ways our lives are much simpler. We can ask ourselves and each other what we want to do and be as individuals. Then we can do our best to become that which we envision and encourage our partners and friends to do the same.

Because I am a mother of three daughters and a stepmother of two sons I am particularly aware of the many varieties of women and men these days. I am hopeful that we can move through the period of our history that finds men and women distrustful of one another and reach a time when we can enjoy whatever differences actually exist.

Strength and character come in two genders
with all kinds of preferences.

The universe begins to look more like a great
thought than like a great machine.

Fritjof Capra

My two stepsons are scientists. One is a physicist. I have never
inquired, even to be polite, what they study. I flunked biology in
college, barely passed chemistry in high school. I have assumed that
I would not understand what either of them might tell me if I asked
them. Besides, I am much more interested in people than in fruit
flies or subatomic particles.

Imagine my surprise, then, when I attended a lecture on chaos
theory and the New Science and understood, I think, most of what
the speaker said. Physics, it turns out, sounds a whole lot more like
theology these days than the scientific method I learned in high
school and college.

We are all, it seems, connected to each other and to the environment. Haven't Native Americans been telling us this for hundreds of
years? My action, physicists might say, will affect not only my group
and my immediate environment but, because of interconnecting
space, will affect groups and environments distances away.

I have heard this before, but not from science. Could these spiritual truths to which we pay so little attention be laws of nature? If
so, then the greed of Wall Street might cause the wars in Eastern
Europe, the graciousness of an individual act of kindness in Indiana
might affect the ability to feed the hungry in Angola.

*My willingness to simplify could affect much more
than my immediate environment.*

—————————— ❦ ——————————

Anger is a reaction to our own
limitations and powerlessness.

Adele J. Gonzalez

—————————— ❧ ——————————

It has been awhile since I was really angry. Usually the passionate kind, the kind that gives me an energy surge, is reserved for
my husband or my children. Those closest to me have the unfortu-
nate privilege of calling forth my deepest rage.

The last episode I recall happened at holiday time. Perhaps it was
inevitable that an unexpected visit from a lifelong friend would push
us over the edge. In my husband's "too-tiredness" he lit into me
about what he saw as my indecisiveness. We were off to the races.

Months later I understand that his anger was about his own
inability to control his friend's schedule and his unwillingness to "just
say no" to the friend's request for a place to stay. My anger was
about my inability to step aside when I see his too-tiredness clearly.

If we understood better that our anger is ours and requires
change from us and not others (necessarily), how much clearer we
could be with others about it.

*My anger can make things clearer if
I know the anger is about me.*

---

*Wisdom is about living harmoniously in the
universe, which is itself a place of order and justice
that triumphs over chaos and employs
chance for its ultimate purpose.*

Matthew Fox

Living harmoniously in the universe may mean using my share (filling my needs), and no more, of the earth's resources. It may mean accepting the seeming chaos of so many things outside my control, with the belief that these things have an order and justice I do not understand. Perhaps some things have meaning beyond my understanding and certainly beyond human blame and reconciling.

Living harmoniously may mean freeing myself of unnecessary baggage so that when opportunity comes, the chance of a lifetime, I can see it clearly enough to grab onto it and ride chance to its reformation of something new.

Harmony, wisdom and acceptance all speak to me of openness, willingness and peacefulness. I will not find these qualities bound up as I am in today's possessions, anxiety and fear about tomorrow.

*Living in harmony with our world calls for different
qualities than succeeding in our culture.*

The heart at rest sees a
feast in everything.

Hindi proverb

It is spring again. As I take my regular walk along the banks of the Mississippi I see men and women in plaid wool shirts fishing, teenagers picking up trash along the path, children on in-line skates and in little houses pushed or pulled by parental runners and bicyclists.

We revel in spring in the Midwest. After months of short cold days and long cold nights, old couples stroll hand in hand in matching "I love Grandma/Grandpa" sweatshirts. Younger singles walk dogs of countless breeds. Runners run. Cross-country skiers ski on things with wheels. There is a mass exodus from the great indoors.

The snow is gone. Green shoots push up through brown grass and the air smells delicious. I need nothing more to make me happy on these first good days than seeing and smelling and listening to the sounds of rebirth. My heart is at rest.

The seasons are a feast for
which my heart waits.

＊

We ascribe beauty to that which is simple;
which has no superfluous parts; which
exactly answers its ends.

Ralph Waldo Emerson

＊

The most beautiful things I have known are places. The most beautiful places I have known are not constructed but discovered, and I have discovered them in my middle age and my second marriage. I can rerun in my mind the rivers and streams of Montana. I can recall water rushing down rocky faces into deep pools or the sun-spattered surface of streams wandering through meadows or woods. A coyote glimpsed only fleetingly one hot afternoon north of Helena returns to my imagination.

My husband introduced me to birds. He finds beauty in any species newly identified. I am drawn particularly to the most gaudy. A cardinal-like bird in Mexico with plum and burnt umber plumes, as well as the fiery red of our own bird, startles me when I see one. The Steller Jay, first seen in the Colorado Rockies, flashes a turquoise and royal crest that makes the more subdued blue jay of my acquaintance dull by comparison.

These mostly quiet places, this beauty remembered and acknowledged, are gifts of a relationship I could not have appreciated in my youth. My quiet husband would not have had enough "superfluous parts" to attract me in my 20s. Yet as I grow with him I am grateful for the real beauty he has shown me.

The loveliness of nature is available at any time
to startle or calm by its simple power.

Why do we always want the things we
cannot have? Why do we not avail ourselves of
those things which we can have for the asking: the
beauty of the countryside, the color of flowers,
the magic of snowflakes, the loveliness of
clouds passing in the sky above us, the sparkle
of the stars shining in the silent night?
Why are we not content with our riches?

Solar Forst

I'll bite, why?

Were we toilet trained too early? Did we fail to resolve some fundamental complexes? Were we reinforced for the wrong things? Did the economic system corrupt us? Are we too busy keeping up with the Joneses? Are we tainted by original sin? Are we just plain greedy? Are we caught in the grips of an existential dilemma? Have we made poor choices? Are we fraught with guilt? Have we learned too well the expectations of the society around us? Have we taken a false turn in our search for meaning?

Would it make any difference if you knew why? Or is wondering why itself another reason not to be content with today's riches?

*Enjoy something you have instead of wishing you
could enjoy something you don't have.*

To care for the living earth is
to care for ourselves.

from a Sierra Club poster

Ultimately the earth is our home. But practically speaking, our abode is our home. Yet our abode sits on the earth and in a community of some sort. We and the community need the earth's air to breathe, the earth's water to drink and the produce of the earth to eat to sustain life.

Many of us rely on the earth for more than basic sustenance. We are re-energized and enriched by being in a special place—by a quiet lake, along a rugged coast, deep in a canyon, on a vast prairie, among the patterns of the desert, in the coolness of a forest. These are places to fill our spiritual needs as well as our physical ones.

We should care for the earth because it is sacred. We should care for the earth because life other than ours depends on it. We should care for the earth for future generations. And, if for no other reason, we should care for the earth so it will sustain us.

When we care for the earth we
are caring for our home.

Each of us weaves a strand in the web
of creation. There is no one else who
can weave that strand for us.

Duane Elgin

Weaving a unique strand of creation involves each of us in the world in two somewhat different ways. First, it implies that we are embodied by creation, that we are a part of—not apart from, above or removed from—creation. We share this kind of involvement with all the other facets of the cosmos; it takes many strands to weave the web.

It also suggests that, though we are part of creation, we also have a part in creating. What we do, or fail to do, has an effect. The course and conduct of our lives are not neutral. We, as individuals and collectively, have an impact and make a difference. What we eat, how we travel, what we tell our legislators, how we dispose of our trash, how we generate electricity—all these things and so many more become part of the web.

What will you weave into your strand? Will you have fibers for people, animals, air, water, plants, rocks, dirt and the other elements of our universe? How will you connect your strand with others?

Today I will be more aware of the
part I play in the web of life.

Wisdom

6

Wisdom

I t is the nature of humans, I think, to gain some wisdom about some things along the way. I don't know anyone (perhaps you do) whom I would describe as wise. I know lots of people I'd describe as having wisdom about some things. My husband is wise in the application of theory to reality. He's often wise about making sense of seemingly senseless environments or situations. I wouldn't describe him as wise about his own emotions, however, or about his management of time. This is just my opinion, you understand.

I have some wisdom about people. Since both my husband and I work with the Myers-Briggs Type Indicator®, I know that my "type" often sees the good in others and is an effective and generous mentor of their growth. This is not universally true. I have sometimes been mean-spirited in my behavior toward my stepchildren and defensive with my own children.

I think I have realistic expectations of others and often encourage them to slow down, relax and smell the raspberries. But I'm not so wise about expectations of myself. I have often found at the end of a summer or a year that I have spent most of my time working and not much of my time relating to the people I love, admiring nature's beauty, pondering my spiritual life or baking bread.

We all have learned some things along the way. Those things can change us in beautiful and terrible ways. The abused child can learn from his abuse that it is the only effective way for an adult to wield power, and therefore becomes himself an abuser. That child can also learn from the same experience to avoid violence and to seek peacefully the resolution of all conflict in his life. It is said so often that it's not what happens to us that shapes our lives but what we think and feel and do about what happens.

Larry and I could be grandparents. Our children are in their twenties and thirties. Some are married and some are not. So far we only have granddogs that frighten our only joint progeny, Solomon the cat. But we are old enough to be wise. Grandparents are often described in literature as wise. We have learned personal lessons about marriage, having each failed at our first. We have learned lessons about parenting and have taught some of those to each other. We have acquired professional knowledge and expertise, which some of our clients might describe as wisdom. We have each lost a parent—our father—who played a significant role in who each of us was and who each of us has become. We are mostly honorable, mostly caring, mostly conscientious older adults who can slide happily into childish silliness and fun. But are we wise? Yes and no.

We write of wisdom or lessons learned along the way because these lessons have been important to us. If some people do not consider these lessons true wisdom, they at least demonstrate endurance. We write of wisdom because each living thing, plant or animal, possesses it. The baby sandhill crane will lift its young bulk off the ground only when it needs to migrate. The child will walk and fall and walk again in unself-conscious learning that we adults might identify as wisdom. The rose opens and shares its fragrance, decays and loses its velvety petals, and dies. It knows when to do these things. And the adult tries to make use of experience, tries to learn the lessons experience teaches in order to survive, to flourish and to encourage others. We write of wisdom because we need to learn life's lessons ourselves and by writing we can sometimes see those lessons more clearly. We share what we have learned in humility, knowing that our learning may not apply to you and that your learning could well help us to grow. We write of this to learn to live more wisely as a part of living simply.

There is much to learn in life, but it is
best to learn how to live.

Jim Rosemergy

We studied many subjects in school and learned many lessons. Our school lessons were about math, history, science and English. The other lessons we learned were about playground bullies, teachers' pets and best friends.

In our education, an important lesson was frequently overlooked—learning how to live. We were seldom taught how to live in harmony with ourselves and others, to value and incorporate balance in our lives and to be deliberate about the things we want to do, experience and influence.

Although we spend much of our formative years learning the lessons of school, the lessons of life most often come through living and through our interactions with others. Fortunately, learning how to live more effectively is always available to us. As long as we are alive and mindful, we can continue to learn life's lessons.

Today I will be open to learning
a lesson in how to live.

—————————————— ❦ ——————————————

Education, I fear, is learning to see one
thing by going blind to another.

Aldo Leopold

—————————————— ❦ ——————————————

It was still dark and cold that early July morning when the members of the nature photography class gently jostled one another for
the best position to shoot the (we hoped) soon-to-appear spectac-
ular Rocky Mountain sunrise. I managed to get a spot where I had
a tree silhouetted in the upcoming rays. And I did shoot many pictures, including one photo that was particularly striking.

Then something (boredom, intuition)—I doubt that I knew then,
and I surely don't remember now—made me wonder what lay
behind us. So I turned away from the view all were so intently
focused on to observe an incredibly rich scene washed in heavy
orange, with a focused streak streaming down as if a sign from heav-
en. I looked where I wasn't directed to and was richly rewarded.

What have you gone blind to and missed by focusing so closely
on what your upbringing, education, job and culture trained you to
see? Have you passed by the beauty and restoring qualities of
nature? Have you overlooked the incredible gift of your loved ones?
Do you ignore people not usually part of your world whom you
have something to share with or learn from?

What can you do today to break the limiting patterns of your
vision and attention? Can you take a new route, speak to people
you usually don't interact with, stop work early to spend time with
a loved one, spend 20 minutes by yourself, do something for someone else, read a poem, go without a meal?

Today I will turn myself around to see a
new possibility in my daily world.

There is no arriving somewhere
without leaving somewhere.

John Updike

Leaving my son at college was difficult for both of us. Wisely he observed, "One day you have your own room, your own house, your own family, your own yard, your own cat. And the next day you don't." Of course, he wanted to go to college—he had spent much time and energy selecting an appropriate one, and even more energy creating a high school record that would allow him to be admitted. He definitely wanted to go, but he didn't want to leave.

Often we are in the process of arriving somewhere different in our lives—a job switch, a different abode, another friend, a new habit. Sometimes change is thrust upon us and we are transported to a new place without being consulted. A death, divorce, business merger or aging body might be the vehicle.

At other times we may long anticipate the positive effects of change with excitement and a sense of opportunity, such as when going off to college, getting married, having children or buying a vacation home.

But for every change—even those we've awaited for so long—there is a leaving. We may be happy to be leaving a stressful job, a house that has required so much of our time, a hurtful relationship. We may also be sad to be leaving friends, a special place, security, even when we know it is time to move on and we want to move on.

*As change comes to my life it is important to
be aware of what I am leaving.*

❧

Just one phone call can
change your life.

from a TV Ad

❧

Some phone calls—or rather the information they convey—do change our lives. They tell of a job offer, a death, a homecoming, a birth.

But the exhortation in this ad was not about that sort of call. It was a call to lose weight dramatically, reap untold wealth with a business scheme, take advantage of an amazingly lucrative investment that has hitherto remained a well-kept secret, or change your life by reading a book or attending a seminar.

That claim is the self-help movement's version of cheap grace. It entices us to believe that important, fundamental shifts can be made by picking up the phone and charging something to our credit cards.

Of course, it isn't that easy—something worthwhile rarely is. Making a phone call or other contact may indeed be a first step on a new part of our journey. But just as insight is not conversion, the first step is not the change.

For me, the challenge usually isn't taking the first step—the remnants of many potential dramatic life changes litter the path of my journey—but rather all the subsequent actions necessary to keep me on track. The discipline of follow-through, keeping on keeping on when the initial excitement has ebbed and the seedling new behaviors have yet to sprout, has been a particular stumbling block for me. How about for you?

Knowing that change takes work can be a source
of strength to me instead of discouragement.

―――――――――――― ❧ ――――――――――――

When the same pattern repeats itself in my
experiences, life may be telling me
that I have homework to do.

Daily Word for July 13, 1992

―――――――――――― ❧ ――――――――――――

Patterns—sometimes called habits—are useful, even necessary. If we all didn't keep the same pattern when driving our cars, playing softball or going through the cafeteria line, confusion and sometimes injury would result. Good patterns, such as exercising regularly or reserving Thursday evenings for a family activity, help us achieve things that are important to us.

But we also have another kind of pattern, one that we maintain even though it delivers unsatisfying results. It keeps occurring but we keep ignoring its consequences or hope that somehow next time the results will be different.

Sometimes the homework we need to do is relatively simple— we become aware of the pattern and begin to modify it. Other times it is more challenging and may require significant effort and dramatic action to alter actions that we seem to have little control over.

When patterns recur, we are being provided repeated opportunities to learn the lessons we need to realize new aspects of ourselves, to become fuller, more complete versions of ourselves.

Patterns we may need to learn from, that may be holding us back from important growth, include repeatedly getting into relationships with people who won't support us in pursuing our dreams, breaking commitments to self or others, abuse of alcohol, drugs or other harmful substances, eating in unhealthy ways, devoting disproportionate amounts of energy to work and directing our anger at others.

*Today I will celebrate my healthy habits and be
more aware of the lessons I need to learn.*

❧

Your mind works like a garden. Everyone knows
if you plant beans, you won't raise potatoes. . . .
Plant negatives, reap negatives.

Zig Ziglar

❧

My family moved a lot when I was growing up, staying as little as six months and not more than two years in any one place. Each time my Dad came home to announce that we were moving, I would begin to create a picture of our new house from the description he gave. I would try to imagine the house and its rooms—especially my room—as well as the yard, street and other houses in the neighborhood.

Of course, I never got the details right because I was making them up. But what I was doing, I now understand, was using my mind to help create a new reality and to ease yet another transition in my life.

We do that all the time—imagine something we are trying to do before we actually do it. A way to help accomplish what you want in your life and to move yourself toward desired goals is to deliberately focus your mind on imagining the results you seek. For example:

- Imagine yourself successfully making an important change.
- Visualize a long-standing conflict or difficult situation being resolved.
- See yourself relaxed on vacation with family and friends.
- Picture yourself eating healthy foods and exercising.

Your mind is already doing this picturing naturally. You might as well put it to work for you by visualizing those things you want to happen in your life.

Today I will sow my mind with images of
what I want to flower in my life.

We cannot live the afternoon of life
according to the programme of life's morning;
for what was great in the morning will be little at
evening, and what in the morning was true
will at evening have become a lie.

Carl Jung

To me it is uplifting to realize that adults continue to develop and grow psychologically throughout their lives, giving more time and energy to particular parts of their lives and personalities when warranted by their current phase of life. For example, becoming established in a career or creating a family usually requires our full attention as young adults.

It also means that some of what was real and important to us earlier in life may be less so now. We may even wonder why we devoted so much energy to some of the things we did when we were younger. Now, different elements emerge to nudge and tug us in fresh directions. To be whole persons, we pay attention to and experience different parts of ourselves.

The exciting news is that we can look forward to this natural unfolding. We can await with anticipation the experience of previously hidden, even undervalued, aspects of self. We have all seen it in others. Someone who has been very outgoing and engaged in the world begins to pull back and explore inner terrain. Another who has been all business begins to work less, softens, perhaps makes time for grandchildren or involvement in the community.

What we have all seen in others will likely come to us. And with the unfolding will arrive opportunities to review, reclaim and redirect.

My continuing unfolding is an opportunity
to increase balance in my life.

---

*"There" is no better than "here." When your
"there" has become a "here," you will simply obtain
another "there" that will again look
better than "here."*

from *The Rules for Being Human*

When we become frustrated, uncertain about where we are headed but pretty sure this isn't it, we need to guard against what has been called the "geographic cure," the solution we are sure will come by picking ourselves up and moving to another job, another relationship, another place. Sometimes, of course, that is exactly what we need because the job has taken much more from us than we are now getting from it or the relationship has turned destructive.

But we also need to remember that we have had a part in those situations that have frustrated and hurt us. If we merely pick ourselves up and move to another place without examining our part, without doing some inner work, we are likely to find ourselves again in a similarly baffling circumstance.

The journey toward simplicity, the life of balance, has a significant inner component. In fact some would say that it is all inner work. When you see someone who has carved out a balanced life and who pursues his own dream, what you are seeing on the outside is no doubt a reflection of inner balance and peace that is the product of long and ongoing work. When we are busy looking for a solution "out there" we may overlook the part of the solution that is "here."

*I will be ready to go "there" when I have
finished my work "here."*

---

*When I was growing up I cannot remember
a single story of an adult whom I was aware of who
had a positive transformative growth experience in
adulthood. And if all the growth that happens is
hidden from you, that's a pretty powerful message.*

Mark Gerzon

I do not remember any stories about the positive transformative experiences of adults either. I don't know if I was just unaware of them, if they were in fact told in my presence and I ignored them or if they were intentionally not shared with youngsters.

What about you? Were you aware of such stories? Were the challenges and opportunities of adulthood presented to you in a positive light when you were a child?

For whatever reason, I entered adulthood quite unprepared for what would happen, unaware of the benchmarks awaiting me on the path ahead. What a joy it is now to know the possibilities of adult development, to view them positively and share them among ourselves. How liberating it is to know that when we live out those patterns, we are not unusual or crazy, but instead are experiencing the kinds of things that many adults experience.

Let us take advantage of opportunities to mentor emerging adults, to introduce them to what we know of the path and not to hide what we have already experienced.

*I celebrate the opportunities for growth
given to me and to all adults.*

Rules are best to guide,
not to dictate.

Ellen J. Langer

Think of the chaos inherent in a world without rules! No office hours to abide by, no schedule for meals, no need to get dressed in the morning, no need to say thank you, no need to drive on the right side of the road. Even in those moments when we long for fewer rules and more freedom, we would probably admit that some rules are needed to make life in a community livable.

When rules are made to guide the effective meshing of families, organizations and cultures, they are helpful and even freeing. When they are made by individuals and countries to protect themselves and exclude or put down others they are binding and diminishing. When there are innumerable rules governing the most specific of behaviors, more energy must be expended to follow the rules, allowing less energy to create a better family, organization or country.

Simplifying our lives involves paring down the rules to a minimum and learning to see them as guides rather than dictates for self and others.

What rules are important to me now?
What flexibility might I learn concerning those rules?

The only thing that makes life possible is
permanent, intolerable uncertainty:
not knowing what comes next.

Ursula Le Guin

"Permanent, intolerable uncertainty" doesn't seem like much of a prescription for happiness. I would much rather have semipermanent, tolerable certainty as long as I get to say what that is. Yet even when I am sure I know what comes next, it doesn't.

The child I nurtured and related to with such ease suddenly rejects me in her adulthood. The job I thought I would have until retirement crumbles beneath me. Strangers help me get through hard times. And the stepson who long ignored me suddenly seeks my opinion.

Whereas once I wanted lavish surroundings, now I want the simplest of settings. Whereas talent once seemed a burden I had to spread as widely as possible, now I want to apply it carefully to deep interests. Whereas hard work was once the highest good, now laughter and loving are my ideals.

Perhaps intolerable uncertainty is not such a bad thing after all. As I change, so do others. If I can welcome the uncertain, then perhaps I will be open to the grace inherent in my own and all other lives.

I encourage intolerable
uncertainty as the status quo.

When the pupil is ready the
teacher will appear.

Native American saying

At one serious turning point in my life, I realized that I had
been behaving in a way that was growth retarding rather than
growth enhancing. When I told a group of supportive friends of
this revelation, they all smiled and affirmed that my assessment of
my own behavior was accurate. But they all also affirmed that I had
heard this assessment from others before. At the time I could not
believe that I had been privy to this wisdom prior to my own discovery of it.

Now I recall that I had been told by quite a few family members,
friends and teachers. But the pupil wasn't ready. I wasn't ready to
give up a way of being that had power for me. Only when I was
ready could I see the wisdom of letting it go, and only when I could
see that wisdom could I accept the help of people who knew better than I how to bring about this personality shift.

As I move from acquiring to maintaining to divesting myself of
things in my life, I am finally ready to be taught to live with less. I
want less obligation, less stress. I am not sure how to make room
for this, but I am ready for the teacher to appear.

As I become ready to understand how to change,
those who can best teach me will appear.

---

*Celebration of passages provides an opportunity
for people to remember stories of the
experience being observed and to
draw new insights from them.*

United Church of Christ Book of Worship

A recent wedding provided me the opportunity to remember my own, both of them. One took place when I was very young; at least I seem to my older self to have been very young then. It was arranged by my mother and attended mostly by my parents' friends and my husband's family. The other took place when my children were almost adults and my husband and I arranged it.

The wedding I recently attended evoked memories of both of my own weddings. I was young. I was not so young. My first mother-in-law was dour. My present mother-in-law is a treasured friend. I was married by a priest. I was married by two ministers, one a woman and the other my husband's best friend. The older me celebrated with a joy unknown to the younger me.

Celebrations mark our birth, our growth and our aging. Happy and sad recognitions of blessings or grieving bring life's cycles into focus, activate memory and anticipation. What richness celebrations add to family history. The passages they mark draw us closer in remembering our own similar passages.

*The marking of a special day forms a core
from which rays of memory emanate.*

————————————— ❦ —————————————

Why is it that we tend to dwell upon
the troubles others have caused us, and to fail
to notice and to forget quickly the
inconvenience and trouble we cause them?

David Reynolds

————————————— ❧ —————————————

One of my adult daughters challenges my behavior with great regularity. She wants me to be honest when I would rather hedge. She wants me to pay full attention when I would rather do two things at once. I begged her recently to give me the same benefit of the doubt she gives her friends. She responded, "What makes you think I treat my friends any differently than I treat you?" Wow! Think about the troubles she causes them!

It is mighty annoying not to get respect from her. I have spent a lot of energy ranting about how I raised her as a single mother, and how she ought to be grateful for all the sacrifices I made. She ought to like me even though I do not like her very much right now.

The truth is that I have had expectations for this child, that she should change in some way, for most of her life. What a drag for her! If I can remember the inconvenience and trouble (not to mention pain and fury) those expectations caused a very capable young woman, perhaps I can get over her frequently legitimate gripes and get on with my own life.

*Selective memory can lead to blaming and
blaming can be a great reason not to
shape our lives as we want them.*

Know that humility, authority, rebuke,
exhortation, compassion, freedom of speech,
kindness, severity, in a word everything,
has its own time.

Basil

Some years ago I sat among a new group of women, apprehensive about my place in the group and a little lonely because of my newness. Very early in my time with them, I knew that I wanted what one of the leaders of the group seemed to have: self-confidence. She had, of course, developed this apparent confidence over quite a few years, and through lots of testing and mistake making. I wanted it immediately.

Now, almost ten years after I left that group, I have made many changes in my life that have required that I trust myself, that I have self-confidence. I did not acquire it overnight, and I am not sure when I began to trust myself. But that trust was, at least in part, learned from watching the leader of that women's group.

I am frequently impatient or discouraged as I try to change the course of my life to include more time for meditation, more writing and less busyness. Time contains the process of which I am hardly aware. I will only recognize myself after the fact—when the products of this process of change are visible.

There is a time for everything. It is my job to
move the process toward the thing
I want, whose time will come.

Growth requires engagement with difference
and with people embodying
that difference.

Jean Baker Miller

To grow, every living thing must change and be exposed to change. Engagement with difference is a requirement of being alive. But we can engage with difference gracefully, with fear, resentment, anticipation, with any number of emotions.

Much of our engagement with difference just seems to happen. An adolescent brings home a girlfriend or boyfriend whose difference causes us to examine our own prejudices. A new co-worker's difference causes us to look at previously unexamined behavior. Differences can be physical, economic, environmental or social.

Sometimes we engage willingly. A change in lifestyle, a new neighborhood, a decision to let go of things that have previously provided a sense of security; all of these require us to engage with difference, and all encourage growth. Even when we engage hesitantly or reluctantly, the engagement will cause us to grow.

As I choose to release possessions, schedules
and titles, I know that I am growing.

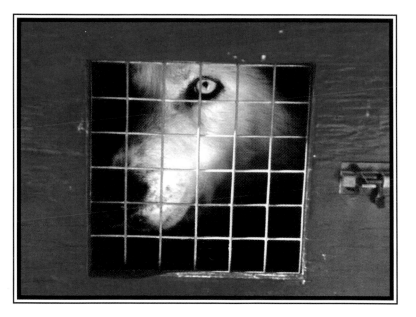

---

*Any form of egocentricity, of selfishness,
obscures your deeper self and blinds
you to how things happen.*

John Heider

In my youth I believed that everything I thought was important to everybody. People I was close to disappointed me, of course, when they did not find important those things I held dear. I chalked up those times to others' inferiority. Really. How egocentric can you get?

When I began to learn about personality differences in my 30s, I realized that many people attach little importance to what I deem significant. It was surprising to discover such diversity in what makes people want to get up each morning. Still, I had some sense that the world revolved around my perceptions.

Very rarely can I stand outside that orbit whose gravitational pull is my self. But for the split seconds I can, I see a much richer landscape, a much deeper universe, with other orbits around other selves and much more. Those seconds are the light that illuminates reality, contrasting the usual darkness of my ego. When the vastness is apparent, my own needs and perceptions are proportionate to the needs of other persons, trees, rivers and rocks. And all is right with all of it.

*Moments of light can change
lives of darkness.*

---   ⚜   ---

Learn to see things backwards,
inside out and upside down.

John Heider

---   ⚜   ---

If we stand in only one place, we see only what can be seen from that perspective. When I move my bed from one place in my bedroom to another, I look out a different window onto a different street, into different trees and sky.

Seeing things backwards or upside down means risking another perspective. If we have a great deal invested in seeing the world one way and something happens to cause us to question that view, the questioning can be painful. How much more fun it might be to move our internal beds intentionally every once in awhile. What would happen if I decided my mother really does try to show me her love? What would change if I gave a tenth of my income to a cause or agency that benefits my community? If I choose to live with less, from what do I free myself? To what new thing might I bind myself?

I can still remember swinging by my knees from a big tree in my backyard. My world was literally upside down. I could see the cobwebs clinging to the underside of the picnic table, the little animals darting head down and feet up into the stone wall I hardly ever noticed. My hair swung beneath me and eventually my head hurt. Each time, when I would finally haul myself upright onto the branch from which I had hung, it would take a dizzying moment to reorient myself.

How would I see my life if I looked at it
backwards or upside down?

I know my faults so well that I pay them small heed.
They are stronger than I am.
They are me.

Florida Scott-Maxwell

Part of learning to live in harmony with each other and the earth is learning to accept ourselves with our particular traits and tendencies. Each of us has gifts that we and the world can celebrate. And each of us has dark recesses we are at least occasionally ashamed that we have.

As part of learning to live fully, we learn not to run from those recesses, but to begin to explore them tenderly. What we once thought of as a fiery temper may now appear as a passionate nature. The painful shyness that plagued our youth may now be a contemplative temperament. To move the world toward peace and harmony we need both passion and contemplation.

Those parts of us that we saw as faults may now be seen as strengths. This does not mean that violence and greed are behaviors to nurture. Anything we do that intentionally diminishes another diminishes us as well. It does mean that our dark sides are but the polar opposite of the gifts we show the world. To simplify our lives we can accept the whole continuum. When those "faults" are so much a part of us that they are us, we can begin to see them as blessings.

I can tenderly explore the dark reaches of my
soul to bring more of myself to the light.

I discovered that there is all the difference
in the world between knowing something
intellectually and knowing it as
"lived experience."

Joanna Field

As children many of us distrusted our parents' advice, which
came from their experience. How many times did we think to ourselves, "I can handle staying out late," or, "Mom doesn't know my
friend as well as I do"? How many times did we prove our parents
right in our own "lived experience"?

As we age, though, it may be important to prove or disprove our
own and our advisors' intellectual knowledge. Sometimes that
knowledge is just assumption. If we thought we would be happy
scrambling for a top position in our profession and find instead that
we are losing our internal balance as well as our sense of humor,
perhaps our lived experience indicates that greater satisfaction may
be found in simpler pursuits.

In trusting the messages that come from our experience we will
constantly fine-tune our course through life, so that what we
thought was so can be amended by what we experience as so for
ourselves. Each lived experience will add a measure of confidence
that we can go on discovering who and what we mean to be.

Knowledge lays the foundation
for lived experience.

—————————— ❦ ——————————

Nothing which is true or beautiful or good
makes complete sense in any immediate
context of history; therefore we
must be saved by faith.

Reinhold Niebuhr

—————————— ❦ ——————————

The kindness expressed by someone I hardly know, at a time when no one knows how much I need it; the haunting melody played somewhere near, perhaps from the next apartment; the child who looks at me with absolute trust; none of these makes sense in the moment. Yet they occur. Minor miracles are repeated every day.

The happiest people I know seem to expect these unexpected moments, these absolute signs of goodness, and are delighted rather than surprised. They seem mostly to be at peace with life, although not necessarily placid. In fact, some are passionate about everything from politics to Parcheesi. Most of the people I know who are like this are grandfathers and great-aunts, older people. And most of them have had plenty of reasons to lose faith in life. But they haven't.

I want to cultivate this faith by concentrating on the goodness, the beauty and the truth all around me. When I hear an honest statement, uttered at the expense of popularity, witness a good deed done without expectation of gratuity, see a beautiful flower, hear a lovely song, smell a rapturous aroma, I will remind myself that these represent faith in my life.

The cruelty, pettiness and dishonesty of much of our culture are real and present. However, they stand beside goodness and truth. Today I choose faith that goodness will reveal itself.

―――――――――――――― ❧ ――――――――――――――

i am on the other side of the rainbow/
picking up the pieces of days spent waitin for
the poem to be heard/ while you listen/
i have other work to do.

Ntozake Shange

―――――――――――――― ❧ ――――――――――――――

At various times we grow beyond what we have done and perhaps continue to do. We no longer need to prove we are compe-
tent, yet we may go on proving it without realizing that we
continue. We may stay in a job, in a relationship, in an apartment
beyond the time we are happy in them.

The trick in life, at least one of them, is knowing when to move
on. It takes courage to move, to let go, to welcome the void, to prepare for the new. It is frightening to step away from the familiar,
even more frightening to be pushed away by divorce, death, job ter-
mination or accident.

To trust that we have other work to do—that the poem we have
written or the friendship we have made is not the poem we will
write or the friendship we will make in the future—takes courage
and faith. It takes courage to explore our own growth and faith that
that growth will flower, will produce new poetry, new friendship.

I will pay attention to the other side of the rainbow.
I will walk toward it, not without
fear, but in spite of it.

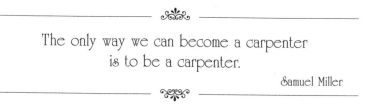

The only way we can become a carpenter
is to be a carpenter.

Samuel Miller

By picking up a saw and sawing a piece of wood (being a carpenter), one becomes a carpenter. We probably will not produce clean edges or an even cut the first time, but by cutting the wood and fitting lengths together over and over we improve our carpentry skills. If we are to grow and develop in work we deeply care about, we must continue to practice skills. Being what we want to be leads to becoming what we want to be.

For many years I have wanted to be an author. I wrote articles for various publications, but nothing longer than ten or twenty pages. An academic course required that I write a book-length paper. By writing that paper I learned that I can write a book. That paper may be a book, but whether it is or not, the process of writing it taught me that I am an author. Now I must continue to practice my author skills to be an author.

If we are to become kind human beings, we must practice kindness; if we are to be singers, we must sing; if we are to excel in any facet of our lives, we must begin awkwardly, practice persistently and reap the rewards of our continuous effort.

When I am impatient with my skills, I will remind
myself that the more I practice that skill, the more
I will know myself as one who has it.

Sometimes the problem is financial, but the
solution isn't money. It's something else—maybe
a life lesson that can only get our attention
through our pocketbooks. If we keep looking
at the money, we may miss the lesson.

Melody Beattie

Not long ago I left a job under a great deal of pressure. For several reasons the job had been very stressful. I stayed because I believed I had a contribution to make and because I did not think I could survive without the paycheck.

Now I have no paycheck and no stress. This is not necessarily a general rule. The stress of no paycheck can be real and preoccupying. But in this case, the life lesson appears to be that it is time for me to do what I really want to do and not what I can get the world to pay me to do. I expect to eventually find a way to get paid for what I want to do. For now I will practice doing it.

Many of the lessons of our pocketbooks are not about money. Oh, money may be the immediate need. And it is simplistic to say that money is not ever the underlying lesson. Still, many problems that present themselves as financial have solutions that are about our attitudes, our values and our goals.

*Let me examine my problems to make sure
that the seeds of my happiness are not
hidden in my pocketbook.*

---

*Rather than pray *for* the things I need, I have
begun to pray *about* the things I need.*

Macrina Wiederkehr

Isn't it wonderful to have that occasional flash of insight that leads directly to attitude and/or behavior change? Praying or meditating *about* the things I think I need is very different than praying *for* them. I don't really know, after all, that I need whatever it is that I am praying for. I might need something else more, or need the thing I think I need only for the briefest moment. If I pray about it, though, my need becomes clear—eventually.

Praying or meditating about something assumes I do not have all the answers. Prayer only gets me into trouble when I think I do have those answers. When I pray about a need, I can hold that need in my consciousness, explore options about that need, think of people I know—or don't know—who can fill the need, and imagine a reduction or increase in the need. All these ways of thinking leave the fulfillment of the need to time, the universe, God, my family, chance or all of the above. It takes me away from trying to control the fulfillment of the need.

Do I really know if the job I want is the right job? Do I know if the prospective partner I have identified will interest me so much in a year, a month? Do I need a new coat, another apartment? Perhaps I really do. Perhaps my needs are real and immediate. If after I have done all of the things I can think of to meet a need, I pray about it, then I accomplish three things. I calm my anxiety. I expand my ability to see choices. I let go the reins of control. Life is much sweeter under these conditions, whether or not my need is met.

*When I become anxious about my needs, I will
find a quiet place and pray about them.*

I leave myself by not believing in my gifts, by comparing myself to others, by allowing discouragement to control me.

Macrina Wiederkehr

There are times when I believe in everyone and everything but myself. When I compare my accomplishments to others, I am sometimes tempted to stop believing in my own gifts. This happens particularly when I am impatient with my own process or when I am unsure of my abilities in new activities.

Meditation often brings me back to a peaceful place within myself where I can embrace my core beliefs in wholeness and simplicity. Meditation can restore the lightness I seek in my interaction with the world and the belief in a divine being that connects me to all beings.

When I am both at ease with the world and at rest in my faith, I am thoroughly at home in my own self.

Meditation brings clarity and
serenity to my life.

This country needs more wise and courageous
shepherds and fewer sheep.

Marian Wright Edelman

When I am accused by colleagues or advisors of moving too quickly, it is important to pay attention to their concerns and their fears. Sometimes I do move too quickly and I am sorry later. It may be important to amend the plan or the timetable. It is equally important, however, to pay attention to my own wise and courageous shepherd and to know that no new idea meets with total approval. No change comes without struggle.

The wise and courageous shepherds of our time, Martin Luther King, Jr., John F. Kennedy, Marian Wright Edelman, have all been flawed human beings. But they have had the courage and the wisdom to stand by their ideals. Because of them and people like them we move our world a little closer to peaceful coexistence with each other and with nature.

Each of us has courage and wisdom. It may not be called forth every day. There will be moments, however, in which we will have opportunities to speak the truth, to be shepherds, instead of more sheep. These moments are precious.

*I appreciate the opportunities to speak the truth,
to offer ideas that will move the world a
little closer to peaceful existence.*

---

*We search, on our journeys, for a self to be,
for other selves to love, and
for work to do. . . .*

Frederick Buechner

For a very few the search reveals self, other loved selves and meaningful work early on. For these few, much of life is a deepening or enhancing of the choices originally made. For many others the search is lifelong for one or all of these goals, and so the self changes, perhaps the selves we love change, and the work we want to do changes as our selves change.

Regardless of where the journey takes us or how we travel, we are not the same toward the end as we were at the beginning. We have been both battered and embraced by life's experiences and we have responded to them differently as experience has been a teacher. Even those people we know about whom we say, "Doesn't she ever learn . . . ?" do learn. It takes some longer than others, and some of us learn some things and resist others.

One of the ways to begin to live simply, if that is a direction we take on our journey, is to open ourselves to the learning life provides. Opening joyfully to what a spouse or a parent or a colleague has to teach us saves so much mental energy that might be wasted on defending ourselves. Remember, though, that what we learn may not be what the teacher intends to teach.

*I am open to divine messages brought
to me in human form.*

Anything will work if you just do it.

Larry Demarest

My wife was praising a new book she was devouring. It was one of those books that takes you through a process of clarifying what is personally important in life and then planning how to alter your life so you can focus on manifesting those important things. It captured her imagination.

"This is really good," she said to me. "Do you think it will work?"

"Anything will work if you just do it," I blurted out.

Though that is probably somewhat of an exaggeration, it isn't far off target. Most exercise programs and machines will work if we will use them. Most sensible approaches are effective when we apply them over and over.

It isn't that there's one best—or magic—book, program, approach or teacher out there that will work once we find it. Rather, what will do it is faithful and consistent application of one of the many approaches that are available. The "D" word—discipline—is the catalyst for success.

When I want to change, I will choose a program
that fits me and follow it.

❦

The quest for certainty blocks the search
for meaning. Uncertainty is the very condition
to impel man to unfold his powers.

Erich Fromm

❦

A friend told me long ago that I was least attractive when I was
most defended. What I think he meant was that I am not warm or
loving, not even available to other people I love, when I am protecting a strong belief or conviction. I defend it so firmly that I seem
to have a shield around me that I can't see over or past. I can't let
another belief in, or even consider another perspective. This happens to me when I am afraid, perhaps afraid of attack, surely afraid
of losing some perception of myself.

As I grow older, I find that I shield myself less and less. I don't
think this is necessarily wisdom but maybe just "nothing left to
lose," as Janis Joplin used to croon. I am less and less sure that I
know anything unconditionally, except that I love a few people that
way. It is less important to me that anyone find me intelligent, witty,
creative or impressive. Perhaps this uncertainty is a kind of power.
Certainly it makes life lighter and simpler.

To approach life uncertainly allows
life to surprise me every day.

———————————— ⚜ ————————————

Nothing we say will be fixed for all time.
Next year, or next week, we will have to find a new,
more appropriate expression of our
experience and our faith.

Christine Lundy

———————————— ⚜ ————————————

The above quote is from a Quaker periodical and refers to the lack of universal applicability of the wisdom or experience of writers and thinkers. What someone wrote two hundred or two thousand years ago about something may or may not be true about that something today. To depend on its truth, indeed to defend ancient wisdom and experience as unimpeachable, is to ignore new evidence and new experience that indicates different truths.

This is not to say that we must reexamine everything we know about living. Should I wear socks today just because I wore them yesterday? Must I wear a hat just because it is cold outside? We could not function without assuming some things. But assuming too much about people and things prevents exploration and discovery, not to mention an awful lot of fun.

*To re-examine some things I have always assumed
were true might reveal new truths.*

Life isn't all afternoons.
Don MacKenzie

When Don uttered those words, he was a fellow college student who had awakened (no doubt more than once) in the afternoon. Eventually aware that he was missing whatever the morning might have had to offer, he intoned—actually more likely muttered—"Life isn't all afternoons."

As a fairly early riser I don't miss many mornings, but like Don I have habits and patterns that act as blinders to direct me toward some experiences and past others. What parts of life am I missing? Do I work too much and miss out on time for friends, family and leisure? Am I too serious and thereby passing up frivolity and light-heartedness? Do I have habitual practices in what I read, where I vacation or the restaurants I frequent that cut me off from new experiences and perspectives? Do my plans and schedules keep me from the unexpected, unplanned, spontaneous, serendipitous?

Mornings are a highlight of my life, but what am I missing during other times of the day?

I will be open to new experiences by doing
something that pulls me out of my
typical patterns this week.

All the significant battles are
waged within the self.

Sheldon Kopp

When I was younger, I would have rejected Kopp's statement out of hand. I had a pretty clear idea who had caused the problems (not me) and what should be done about them ("they" should change what "they" had been doing). At that time, I believed that the significant battles were to be waged outside of myself.

Later, I could more often acknowledge that I had a part in some problems and their solutions. I may have been actively involved in creating the problem and forging a particular solution, or I may have helped create the situation by being passive and not doing my part.

Now I am occasionally aware that even when I have thought the battle was with someone else, it is actually with myself. When I can so clearly see what "they" are doing, I am really holding a mirror up to myself to examine that very same part of me.

When I rail at the speeders in my neighborhood, I remember that I speed in others' neighborhoods. As I teach others the importance of communicating straightforwardly, I think of the times when I don't. I know that the struggles I face in trying to live more deliberately and simply, to reach places that are important for me to reach, are struggles with me.

What was it that Pogo said?

No problem can be solved from the same
consciousness that created it.

Albert Einstein

I remember very clearly writing the check and tearing off the
return portion of the bill. My husband said, "You better be careful."
He was referring to my partial payment of our very large auto insurance bill. My payment was late and incomplete. Later I found a previous bill indicating I owed less than I had paid that day. "Ha, ha!"
I waved the bill in front of him.

I never read any of the words that were written on the bill. Two
weeks later I received my check from the insurance company with
a note that my insurance had been canceled because of incomplete
payment.

I was and am embarrassed about this. I did not sleep the night I
received this notice. How could I have been so negligent as to let
this happen? How could I drive the hundred-plus miles that I needed to the next day? Why didn't I pay attention?

The truth is that I have become lazy about paying my bills and I
have no excuses. I believed that I was immune to consequences
caused by my barest attention. Although my insurance has been
reinstated after several frantic phone calls to our agent, I have had
to examine my attitude and change it.

*The consciousness that ignores cannot
pay close attention.*

There is no permanent solution.

Price Pritchett

S ome types like to practice their tried and true way everytime. Others like to change their way after doing it once or twice, just for the fun of it. This tends to drive the tried and true types nuts. I have worked for quite a few people who like to do, and like their employees to do, things the same way always. Usually they invented the things and they know from experience the right way to do them.

Don't get me wrong. I think having everybody work from roughly the same guidebook is dandy, even necessary some of the time. But without creativity the old right way becomes the wrong way at some point.

My former boss managed the first program of its kind ten years ago. When I left the company nine years later he would not entertain any adjustments to his successful formula. But the business in which this program functions has changed almost completely over that period of time.

The rule breakers need the rule makers to
maintain consistency; the rule makers need the
rule breakers for innovation.

Confession is often an avoidance
of change.

Lee Silverstein

Do you ever read or hear something that applies uncomfortably well to you? I had just such a reaction to this quote. During the years when I drank too much, I would sometimes confess it to a family member or friend. It was a way to excuse and prolong the behavior that caused me and my family much pain.

Confession is a tactic I have used with other behaviors I do not like. When I spend too much or eat too much, I confess it to people around me as if I have no control over the behavior in the first place. I am confessing a "sin" as if it has me and not I it.

I want to be responsible to myself by stopping the behavior that causes me the most discomfort and even shame. But when I overspend or eat too much sugar, I want to acknowledge to myself that I have fallen short of my own desires, not confess sheepishly to my husband or child, so that I can continue to do those things that are against my health and contentment.

Confession was never meant to remove the remorse, but to lighten the load of guilt. I will try to learn discipline so as to reduce my dependence on confession.

Confession does not get me to
a peaceful friendship with myself.
Self-discipline does.

------------------- ⚜ -------------------

If you knew me yesterday, please do
not think it is the same person that
you are meeting today.

John Powell

------------------- ⚜ -------------------

When we haven't seen someone for quite awhile, we can easily see and acknowledge the changes in them. The rapidly growing child, the maturing college student or the old friend not seen for years come to mind.

But when we are with a person day to day, we don't always recognize the gradual changes that take place. In fact, unless we communicate on a personal—yes, intimate—level, we may not even be aware of those changes. Indeed, changes in perspective, beliefs or feelings may be no more evident than those in physical appearance when we see someone regularly.

Of course we can recognize and greet people without knowing their inner lives are changing. We can work together, be neighbors, play together and, sadly, even live together and still not know that inward part. But to truly know whom we are greeting, we must listen, share and not judge.

*I will try to remember that I may be
meeting a new you every time
we encounter each other.*

In silence we learn to make distinctions.
Those who fly from silence, fly also from distinctions.
They do not want to see too clearly.
They prefer confusion.

Thomas Merton

How often I have chosen confusion over clarity. When my decisions are made in haste, as they frequently are, I have a built-in
excuse for their ineffectiveness. "I did the best I could under the circumstances," I sigh. "I had no time to think about it."

Most of the time the decisions are not critical. It doesn't really
matter whether I do one thing or another. Most of the business decisions I make could be made by anyone in my area. The most important criterion is often timeliness, not wisdom. Still, I wish I could
redecide some of them.

Some decisions depend on percolation time, on just being with
the question for awhile. We have been living with the question of
whether to move to smaller quarters for almost a year. The answer
has not come clear yet. My decision to attend seminary percolated
for eight years. When I decided to go, it was exactly the right time.
When I got there I lived with the question of ordination for a year.

*To be able to make the distinction between
what is expedient and what is best, I often need to
hold the question quietly in my soul.*

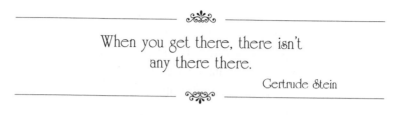

When you get there, there isn't
any there there.

Gertrude Stein

My brother Tom has a new car and a new house. He sends a photo of himself in the car in front of the house. He has worked so hard in so many jobs for so much of his life to be able to afford the house and the car. More important, he has always been a loving and conscientious father, a father who is present to his almost adult children even though he has been divorced from their mother for many years. He is a loving husband (although no saint, I'm sure) and a loving brother and son.

I don't know what this brother would say was his "there." But I bet if you'd asked him when he was 25, "there" would have included the car and the house much sooner than they were in fact a reality. His "there" probably would not have included a divorce, difficult bosses and more than the normal amount of parental anxiety as a loving, noncustodial father.

Tom's "there" is a wonderful place right now. At least it looks that way from here. He smiles broadly from behind the wheel of the big white car in the photo. But Stein's quote cautions that putting too much stock in some future state of having leaves out all the states of being along the way. And it is all the states of being that make us whole.

"There" is a place to dream about.
Here is the place to live.

When it is dark enough, you
can see the stars.

Charles A. Beard

Despair is a strong emotion and an infrequent visitor to my heart. Darkness and despair seem to go together when I have experienced them. As I approach what some would describe as my seniority, I experience the sadness, even the despair of losing youth and facing death.

My mother, a recent widow, writes of despair of a different kind. She has been keeping herself company in the middle of the night, she writes, by inventorying all 52 years of her marriage to my father. She says there were some powerful lows and some wonderful highs. I am sad that she is not sleeping well, but glad that she will share the feelings of letting go of the man she knew best for more than half a century. I read and hear of her despair, the loneliness of living without a man with whom she could at least bicker if not converse peaceably, who kept her warm through most of her nights on this earth.

My mother-in-law tells me I shall discover a wonderful freedom in old age. This must be in my stars. Although I have yet to discover them, I look in the darkness with great anticipation. My mother will let go of both the anger and the joy she knew with Dad and will rediscover her own joy in flowers, grandchildren and the river that runs behind her new home. The dark will reveal its treasures, the tiny rays of light that have been there all along.

Watch over us, stars, until
we can find you.

Everyone is a moon and has a dark side
which he never shows to anybody.

Mark Twain

I don't agree with Sam Clemens here. We think we don't show our dark side to anyone, but many see it anyway. I was surprised in my 30s to find that many of my friends, and even some acquaintances, knew that I spent a good deal of time feeling sorry for myself and blaming others for my perceived misfortunes. I believed that my closest friends saw only my victim and not my whining. I was wrong.

Haven't you been certain that you could solve someone else's problems "if they would only . . . "? The fact that they cannot says more about their own blindness to their dark side than to yours. I know just what my husband, my children and my sons-in-law should do about many things they seem unable to do anything about.

I am poking fun at myself and others here. But I am also serious. We can learn much from others about our dark side if we are willing. This is scary because it asks others to assess our least preferred selves. But this dark side can enrich (I'm not kidding) our whole selves and our relationships with others. When I knew, for instance, that others saw my self-pity, I could decide that it was time to step out of my victim role. Although it was frightening to assume responsibility for my own life, it was also exciting to become more of what I wanted to be.

Dark sides are not invisible but they can be disabling.
Inviting others to reveal them to us can change the
nature of the darkness and of ourselves.

---

*Chance is always powerful. Let your hook
be always cast. In a pool where you
least expect it, will be a fish.*

Ovid

I still read about singers and actors who are instant stars. Just today I read about an 11-year-old who accompanied her older sister to an audition for a major film role. Though she had no intention of auditioning, the 11-year-old was chosen for the role. She later won an award for best supporting actress for the role. If we knew more, I suspect we would find that the girl had had some artistic training. Had she been watching and studying her older sister before this part presented itself?

For years before I became a speaker and trainer, I wanted to be one. I often spoke to groups about subjects in which I had expertise. But I wanted to speak for my supper. Graduate school and one training job—where I spoke about nothing but my subject matter expertise for a year—led to the training and speaking career I now enjoy. I had cast my hook for many years and the fish only bit when I consciously prepared to catch the fish.

So it is with simplifying my life. I am casting my hook and learning to live differently.

We can be whatever we want to be. Whatever that is, it rarely comes to us overnight. But if we prepare, if we consciously make way for the thing we want, we will someday find that we have "caught" it and that it happened just when we were ready for it.

*If you want to change you must prepare for it.
You must bait your hook and cast it into the waters
of becoming. The change will occur—the fish
will be caught—when you are ready.*

It is better to give and to receive.

Bernard Gunther

My education and training have taught me to see dichotomies—to think, observe and speak in terms of "either/or." I learned that it is better to give than to receive. I never thought about the possibility of valuing both. I need to become more aware of seeing such options.

My older son has always been interested in the natural world and the spheres of creativity. As he aged, I suggested that he probably could not do both, that he would have to choose to emphasize one. He graduated from college with two majors—one in biology and the other in art. I no longer speak with him in terms of dichotomies, and I imagine that both science and art will continue to be important in his life.

Yes, it is better to give *and* to receive. It is also better to think *and* to feel, to look at current reality *and* future possibilities, to devote time to work *and* to family, to have a plan *and* to remain flexible.

I can create possibilities by combining rather
than separating and setting things
against one another.

Observe constantly that all things take
place by change. . . . For everything that
exists is in a manner the seed of
that which will be.

Marcus Aurelius

Frankly, I have had enough change for awhile and I don't particularly want to observe it constantly. I want some relief.
Personally, I wish the pace of change in my life would abate. It just
seems to keep coming at us—more work, changes in the lives of
our adult offspring impacting us, the house getting older and needing more attention (my body too!), changes in the neighborhood
and city. Will it ever let up? (I doubt it, I hate to tell you.)

Ironically, much of my income comes from working with groups
that want or need to change. They too are buffeted by wave after
wave of new conditions breaking over them—dramatic changes in
businesses, international competition, Total Quality Management,
working in teams, diversity and so forth. Were it not for change, I
would have to find another way to earn my keep.

So I guess it won't surprise you that I am somewhat ambivalent
about change.

*Change—we can't live without it, but we
don't always have to like it.*

There are many sides of ourselves that
we deny. We are frightened or repulsed
by them and do not want to admit
them into awareness. . . .

Charles Bates

I am only beginning to become aware of those parts of me, the ones that I do not want to acknowledge. For a long time, I simply denied that I had such characteristics. While it was obvious to me that others had them, I must have imagined that I did not.

For example, while some may advocate violent solutions to social problems, I do not. I am not, I would tell myself, a violent person and I believe that violence only begets more violence. More recently I have realized that even though I am not physically violent, I have a violent side that I have not owned. I experience it when I imagine, even hope, that terrible things will happen to people with whom I have conflicts or who commit atrocious acts.

Of course, I argue with myself that my violence (or greed or gluttony or whatever) is different. After all, I may fantasize about violent happenings, but I don't actually carry them out.

Bates counsels that we need to come to terms with these unacknowledged aspects of ourselves in order to take our next steps. In doing so, we are building bonds with other people because we are admitting that we possess the very same characteristics for which we have rejected or denigrated others.

As I am more and more able to acknowledge and accept those parts of myself, I can say, "Welcome to the human community, Larry!"

Acknowledging those previously denied parts
of me is both frightening and hopeful.

--------------------- ❧ ---------------------

This is not the end but our only
place to start from.

James Carroll

--------------------- ❧ ---------------------

This is the end of this book (or at least the last entry). Writing it has been a notable part of our individual paths and our joint journey. We have been challenged to take seriously the learnings of our own experiences, which we have presented here. We can only go forward from here, with new lessons learned and more to come. "Here" becomes "now," which becomes the place from which our next step is taken.

Whatever your journey has been—whether it has already been a considerable one or you are early in the process of recognizing that you are on a journey—we hope these reflections have helped you on your way.

For you, too, today is the only place from which you can go forward. Although we can and must eventually learn from previous events, we cannot alter them. And while we are looking forward to what we hope to create and experience, there are no assurances that we will be granted such opportunities.

And so to live more simply, each day we look for opportunities to walk more gently on the earth: nurturing possibilities for growth for ourselves and others, increasing respect for all life, forging lives of balance and awareness, and creating work that contributes to ourselves and others.

Create well-being for yourself and others,
for all other creatures and
for our earth home.

About the Authors

Sara Orem and Larry Demarest are partners in marriage. They also share many of the same professional interests and activities. Although Sara works for a large corporation and Larry has been a private consultant for eight years, they often partner professionally as trainers, facilitators and course developers of material focused on organizational change. They have five children between them (Sara has three daughters, Larry has two sons) and a beloved cat named Solomon.

Although they are city dwellers, Sara and especially Larry find serenity and renewal in this country's wilderness, particularly the boundary lakes of Northern Minnesota where Larry canoes annually with college chums. There and in other natural places he enjoys bird watching, photographing plants and animals and hiking with Sara.

Sara is a published writer of short stories, artistic reviews, essays and memoirs in addiction to her work in both nonprofit and for-profit organizations. Larry has written for the Center for Applications of Psychological Type and professional and men's journals. This is the first book for Sara and Larry.

Make a move towards positive growth with

THE RECOVERY LIFESTYLE MAGAZINE

Changes

Relationships
Spirituality
Co-dependency
Depression
Money and Work
Sexuality and Intimacy

Body Image
Self-Esteem
Recovery
Physical and Emotional Health
Parenting/Stress
Social Issues

CHANGES, the nation's leading personal growth magazine, is for people who have made a choice to create positive change in their lives.

Order CHANGES today and see why thousands of others consider it to be an integral part of their positive growth plan. Here's our special Growth offer to you: One year of CHANGES for **40% OFF** our basic subscription price of $30 (that's six bi-monthly issues) for **just $17.95**. OR take advantage of our **TWO YEAR**, SUPER PERSONAL GROWTH SPECIAL OFFER of **50% OFF** the basic subscription price of $60. That's right, **pay just $29.95** for twelve bi-monthly issues; **two full years** of informative, inspirational, how-to and hands-on sessions of personal growth.

OUR GUARANTEE TO YOU!

If you are not completely satisfied with the quality of your subscription, for any reason, cancel at any time and we'll refund the difference of the unused portion of your subscription.

Clip and mail this coupon to: Changes Magazine, P.O. Box 609, Mount Morris, IL 61054-0609 or call 1-800-998-0793 for faster service (please mention subscription code RCHC94).

YES!

Please enter my subscription for:
❑ **2 Years (12 issues) of CHANGES for only $29.95 (50% savings)**
❑ **1 Year (6 issues) of CHANGES for only $17.95 (40% savings)**

Name: _____

Title: _____

Address: _____

City: _____ State: _____ Zip: _____

❑ Payment enclosed ❑ Please bill me (U.S. orders only)   QCHC94

Charge my ❑ VISA ❑ MC #: _____

Exp.: _____ Signature: _____

* Basic price: $30.00/yr. FL residents add 6% state sales tax. In Canada, add $7.00 a year for postage. Foreign orders: add $10.00 a year. (US funds only, drawn on US bank.) All Canadian and foreign orders must be prepaid. Please allow 6-8 weeks for delivery.